To the Bitter End

APPOMATTOX, BENNETT PLACE, AND THE SURRENDERS OF THE CONFEDERACY

by Robert M. Dunkerly

EMERGING CIVIL WAR SERIES

Chris Mackowski, series editor
Daniel T. Davis, chief historian

Also part of the Emerging Civil War Series:

To the Bitter End

APPOMATTOX, BENNETT PLACE, AND THE SURRENDERS OF THE CONFEDERACY

by Robert M. Dunkerly

EMERGING CIVIL WAR SERIES

SB
Savas Beatie
California

Second edition, first printing

ISBN-13: 978-1-61121-252-5

Library of Congress Control Number: 2014958739

Published by
Savas Beatie LLC
989 Governor Drive, Suite 102
El Dorado Hills, California 95762
Phone: 916-941-6896
Email: sales@savasbeatie.com
Web: www.savasbeatie.com

Savas Beatie titles are available at special discounts for bulk purchases in the United States by corporations, institutions, and other organizations. For more details, please contact Special Sales, P.O. Box 4527, El Dorado Hills, CA 95762, or you may e-mail us as at sales@savasbeatie.com, or visit our website at www.savasbeatie.com for additional information.

Author's Note:

There have been many good studies of Appomattox, and even of the lesser-known large surrender at Bennett Place, North Carolina, but there has never been an attempt to document *all* of the surrenders in a comprehensive work. This attempts to do that.

Space limited the depth to which any one event could be explored, but each is given equal coverage.

Several points emerged in the course of this research:

- First, the war did not end with a neat closure; its ending dragged on for months in fits and starts.

- Second, the end of the war was very different in each theater—more so than I first realized.

- Lastly, the way the war, and its ending, has been remembered has greatly influenced our understanding and interpretations of it.

— *Robert M. Dunkerly*

Table of Contents

List of Maps

Maps by Hal Jespersen

Acknowledgments

I would like to thank the following for their help with this rewarding project: Series Editor Chris Mackowski; editor Daniel Davis; at Appomattox Court House National Historical Park: Ernie Price, Patrick Schroeder, and Chris Bingham; with Bennett Place State Historic Park: John Guss and Ryan Reed; Chris Calkins of Sailor's Creek Battlefield State Historic Park; author Jeff Toalson; in Mobile: Dr. Ben George and Robert Eddington; with the Citronelle Historical Museum: Alma Johnson and Debbie Odom; Mark Ballard with Jacksonport State Historic Park; Dennis Northcott with the Missouri History Museum; Jana Meyer with the Filson Historical Society; Yvonne Settlemeir with the Clay County AR Judge's Office; Michael Mumaugh with Mansfield State Historic Site; Ken Cook; Mike McBride; Joe Davis with Fort Townson; Shannon Moeck of Cedar Creek and Belle Grove National Historical Park; Preston Ware with the Oklahoma Historical Society; Ansley Wegner of the North Carolina Department of Cultural Resources; Jonathan Jackson with the Virginia Department of Conservation and Recreation; Michael T. Kelly and

Now known as the "Silent Witness," a doll belonging to Lula McLean, daughter of Wilmer McLean, sat in the room where Lee surrendered to Grant. A Union officer who was also there took the doll as a souvenir. In 1993, the family descendants of that soldier returned the doll to Appomattox National Historical Park. (cm)

The Confederate Rest monument, surrounded by 1,100 graves, is a centerpiece of Mobile, Alabama's, Magnolia Cemetery. Mobile National Cemetery sits adjacent. Confederate Gen. Braxton Bragg is among the notables buried at Magnolia. (gm)

Gregory Mertz, both of the National Park Service; and Dave Roth with *Blue & Gray* Magazine. Thanks also Theodore P. Savas.

Special thanks go to Sarah Nance, who endured a whirlwind history tour through the Deep South and assisted with research and editing.

I hope that this under-studied aspect of the conflict will receive greater attention from historians and the public.

For the Emerging Civil War Series

Theodore P. Savas, *publisher*
Chris Mackowski, *series editor*
Daniel T. Davis, *chief historian*
Sarah Keeney, *editorial consultant*
Kristopher D. White, *emeritus editor and co-founder*

Maps by Hal Jespersen
Design and layout by Chris Mackowski

PHOTO CREDITS:
Appomattox Court House National Historic Site (achnhs); Complete Photographic History of the Civil War (cphcw); Daniel Davis (dd); Katy Davis (kd); Department of the Navy (don); Tabitha Donelson-Miller (tdm); Bert Dunkerly (bd); Ben George (bg); Emerging Civil War archives (ecw); Historical Marker Database/Tom Daoust (hmdb.org/td); Historical Marker Database/Jim Evans (hmdb.org/je); Historical Marker Database/Stanley and Terrie Howard (hmdb.org/sth); Historical Marker Database/Richard E. Miller (hmdb.org/rem); Chris Mackowski (cm); Mike McBride (mm); Greg Mertz (gm); Shannon Moeck (sm); National Archives (na); National Park Service (nps); North Carolina Department of Archives and History (ncdah); North Carolina Museum of History (ncmh); Oklahoma Historical Society (ohs); Old-new-orleans.com (ono); Dave Roth, Blue & Gray Magazine (dr/b&g); Smithsonian Institution (si); Virginia Dept. of Conservation and Recreation (VDCR); Wikipedia: "Josephine Shaw" (w/js)

Valor Alone

PROLOGUE
APRIL 1865

Spring unfolded with cool temperatures and heavy rains that April. Across the Confederacy, people wondered what the future held. Would their crops produce a good harvest? Could they stretch their money for badly needed new clothing? Would they ever have enough to eat again?

Many were determined to resist, but there were internal cracks in Confederate society. Strong anti-war movements in lower Mississippi, central North Carolina, and other places threatened to undermine the war effort.

By the dawn of 1865, the Confederacy could not make, move, or maintain anything. Its infrastructure was decayed or heavily targeted; its economy in a shambles. Confederate armies controlled only small, isolated areas. Union forces had driven wedges between them, disrupting not only their ability to support each other, but to draw supplies or use transportation networks.

The systems upon which the war effort depended— to raise and train men, to move supplies, to manufacture weapons and ammunition, to pay soldiers, to deliver mail—had all broken down.

There is a tipping point at which a losing side can signal the end of fighting with its forces intact, still able to fight, giving it more strength at the negotiation table. To understand this, we can look to more recent examples of conflicts that had similar endings.

In 1918, Germany crumbled from within, wracked by political division, civilian unrest, and economic collapse. On the Western Front, German troops still held large areas of France and Belgium when the Armistice

The waters of Hampton Roads look peaceful from the shoreline, but major obstacles to peace stood in the way of peace negotiations there in February 1865. (tdm)

LEFT: President Lincoln looked forward to the ending of the war, yet he would not live to see its final conclusion. (loc) RIGHT: Secretary of State William Sewerd was a key partner in planning wartime strategy. (loc)

was signed. The German army marched home under its own power, still a capable fighting force.

The next war ended differently, though. In 1945, Allied forces overran Germany itself. The country was largely occupied, and there was no way to continue the war.

The situation in 1865 was analogous to that of 1945: the Confederacy was overrun, with its opportunity to negotiate a peace or keep its armies in the field long past.

Perhaps the point of no turning back had come in early February at Hampton Roads, where a failed peace conference set the tone for the rest of the conflict.

In the winter of 1865, President Abraham Lincoln sent a feeler to Richmond to gauge the possibility of a negotiation. That intermediary, Francis P. Blair, Sr., proposed to Jefferson Davis that the two sides fight against the French, who had invaded Mexico, and afterwards could then find common ground to resolve the current struggle. French intervention in Mexico had been source of interest and concern to both the Union and Confederate governments. Even soldiers in the ranks of both armies discussed the idea of invading Mexico to oust the French.

Politicians on both sides of the Potomac were feeling pressure as the war dragged on and found themselves willing to talk, yet they were not quite ready to compromise on their views on Southern independence. It is a point to ponder whether the two sides would have met at all had not Blair pushed the Mexican idea. It was likely not intentionally deceitful, but it did bring the two sides to the table.

So it was, on February 3, 1865, on board the *River Queen* anchored at Hampton Roads, Virginia, that

Lincoln and Secretary of State William Seward met with three representatives of the Confederacy: Vice President Alexander Stephens, Senator Robert T. Hunter, and Assistant Secretary of War John A. Campbell. Stevens was a political foe of Jefferson Davis and had been largely inactive during the war. Hunter, a former Speaker of the House, was an experienced Virginia politician. Campbell, a moderate who had initially opposed secession, was a former Supreme Court Justice.

Davis had sent his three representatives with the intention of negotiating a ceasefire and combining efforts against Mexico, yet the Southern delegates were rudely awakened within minutes of meeting Lincoln and Seward. They were caught off guard when the president and his secretary insisted on reunification, not negotiations based on the premise of creating two separate nations, and they showed little interest in Mexico.

Seward then shared news of the XIII Amendment's passage, which outlawed slavery. Yet slavery was not the deal breaker. Lincoln explained he was willing to compromise on slavery, allowing for gradual emancipation and even considering compensation for the value of slaves. Lincoln suggested that the Southern states might "avoid, as far as possible, the evils of immediate emancipation" by ratifying the amendment "prospectively, so as to take effect—say in five years."

However, Stephens, Hunter, and Campbell insisted on Southern independence, making the goals of the two sides mutually exclusive. To the shocked trio of Confederate representatives, there was nothing they could agree to. Campbell wrote: "We learned in five minutes that the assurances to Mr. Davis were a delusion, and that union was the condition of peace."

LEFT: **Confederate Vice President Alexander Stephens was a bitter political foe of Confederate President Jefferson Davis.** (loc) CENTER: **Robert Hunter was a long-time Virginia politician who had served in the House and Senate and was even nominated for president before the war.** (loc) RIGHT: **John Campbell, the Confederate assistant secretary of war, had previously served in the Georgia and Alabama legislatures.** (loc)

On February 3, 1865, the Hampton Roads Conference took place on the River Queen in an unsuccessful attempt to negotiate an end to the conflict. Later, President Lincoln met with Generals Sherman and Grant, and Admiral David D. Porter to discuss the war's final campaigns. (cphcw)

Lincoln and Seward denied that they were demanding "unconditional surrender." Seward said that rejoining the Union could not "properly be considered as unconditional submission to conquerors, or as having anything humiliating in it."

Lincoln stated, "As to peace, I have said before, and now repeat that three things are indispensable:

The restoration of the national authority throughout the United States. . . . No receding by the Executive of the United States on the slavery question. . . . No cessation of hostilities short of an end of the war, and the disbanding of all forces hostile to the government."

The failed conference had great consequences on the remainder of the war, and has generally been overlooked in Civil War scholarship. Across the South, starting with Davis himself, the stance of Lincoln was misinterpreted. The insistence on reunification, rather than working towards a treaty for independence of the South, was seen as a demand for unconditional surrender.

As news filtered across the South in the days and weeks following the meeting, its implications became clearer to civilians and soldiers alike. Richmonder Henri Garidel noted, "Everyone in Richmond is talking about the peace commissioners today, the Yankees and our own. We will see how this all turns out." In South Carolina, Mary Chesnut wrote, "our commissioners . . . were received by Lincoln with taunts and derision. And why not? He has it all his own way now."

Sallie Putnam in Richmond noted:

President Lincoln positively refused to listen to any proposal that had in view a suspension of hostilities, unless based upon the disbandment of the Confederate forces. He refused to enter into any negotiation on any other basis than "unconditional surrender." The hopes of peace that had been for a long time entertained were thus effectually crushed. The expectations of the majority, as to what would be the result of this conference, were fully realized. Every avenue of peace now being exhausted, except such as might be conquered by our arms, a fresh attempt was made to rally the people to a determined war feeling.

"New life was visible everywhere," The Richmond *Examiner* noted on February 16. "If any man talks of submission, he should be hung from the nearest lamp post." J. B. Jones, who worked in the War Department noted, "Valor alone is relied upon now for our salvation. Every one thinks the Confederacy will at once gather up its military strength and strike such blows as will astonish the world." A large public meeting in the city confirmed the attitude at large among the civilians: resist at all costs.

In Tennessee, Abbie Brooks wrote, "Let the South be extinct before she is degraded." Kate Cumming, a nurse in Mobile, Alabama, noted that there was a "large, enthusiastic meeting" soon after the conference. She said, "It is rumored that vice-president Stephens has said he is fully convinced that there is but one way to have peace, and that is to conquer it."

So, it appeared, the Confederacy was willing to fight on, determined to find resolution on the battlefield rather than at the negotiation table. While never stated as actual policy, it seems this mentality was largely accepted by the government, military, and the public at large. Perhaps too much had happened by February 1865. The war had gone on too long—too much blood and treasure had been spent to turn back now and face defeat.

As historian Steven Woodworth noted, "For a large number of Southerners even as late as the beginning of 1865, no peace settlement that included such an arrangement could be considered preferable to continued resistance, however remote the chances."

WELCOME

HISTORI

APPOMATTOX

COUNTY

ATION REUN

"We do not know whether armed resistance is over or whether we are to fight on to the biter end."

— *Kate Stone, May 20, 1865*

"[O]fficers of the division were steadfast to the bitter end."

— *Col. Winchester Hall, 26th Louisiana, May 19, 1865*

(cm)

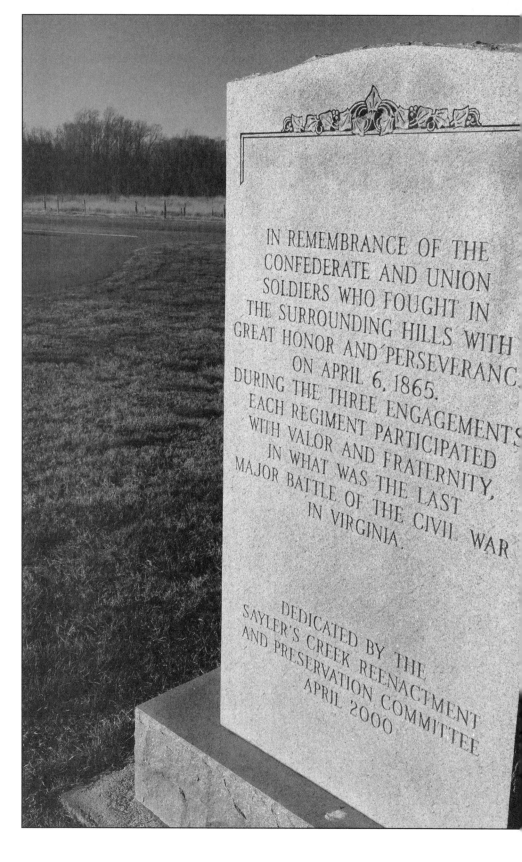

IN REMEMBRANCE OF THE
CONFEDERATE AND UNION
SOLDIERS WHO FOUGHT IN
THE SURROUNDING HILLS WITH
GREAT HONOR AND PERSEVERANC
ON APRIL 6, 1865.
DURING THE THREE ENGAGEMENTS
EACH REGIMENT PARTICIPATED
WITH VALOR AND FRATERNITY,
IN WHAT WAS THE LAST
MAJOR BATTLE OF THE CIVIL WAR
IN VIRGINIA.

DEDICATED BY THE
SAYLER'S CREEK REENACTMENT
AND PRESERVATION COMMITTEE
APRIL 2000

The Grueling Road West

CHAPTER ONE
APRIL 2-8, 1865

The rumble of explosions worried the residents of Richmond's Church Hill neighborhood, as well as those along the New Market Road just south of the city. Soon, flames lit the sky of downtown as the city descended into chaos. After four years of holding off Union armies, the end had come. The capital of the Confederacy was being evacuated.

Government offices hastily packed their supplies and documents, or burned them. Civilians began to flee, or hunker down and wait for the dreaded Yankees to arrive. "All that Sabbath afternoon," Ella Weisiger recalled, "pillows, blankets, necessary clothing and medicines were packed in a large trunk and strapped to the back of our . . . carriage, while bountiful provisions were packed in baskets. All night long father and mother worked securing valuable papers, jewelry and family silver. Mother made bags of unbleached cotton, attached to belts for us to wear under our dresses . . ."

With his lines stretched to the breaking point, Gen. Robert E. Lee had no choice. On April 1, Union troops had crushed Lee's Confederates at the Five Forks crossroads west of Petersburg, then followed up with a general assault all along the lines the next day. "The ground was covered with dead bodies," lamented Pvt. John Coleman of the 6th South Carolina. To save the army, and hopefully continue the war, Lee had to withdraw. Their ultimate destination was North Carolina, to link up with the other Confederate army there.

A monument to the soldiers of both armies stands outside the Sailor's Creek Battlefield Visitor Center. (cm)

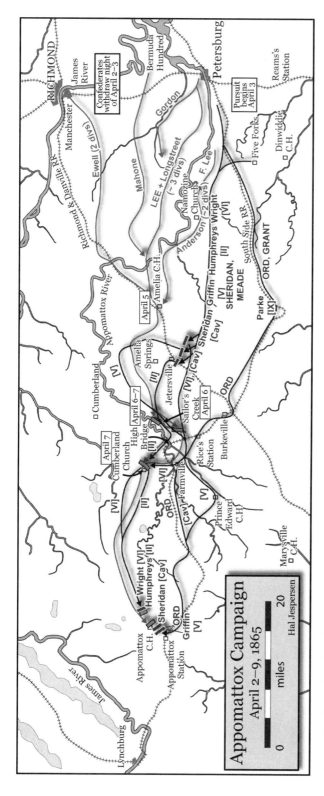

Appomattox Campaign—The Appomattox campaign involved a complicated series of movements and several skirmishes and battles. Three Union armies eventually converged on Appomattox, trapping the Army of Northern Virginia: the Army of the Potomac, Army of the James, and Army of the Shenandoah.

After nine months of static, dull trench warfare, the army was suddenly on the move. Men and animals, emaciated and unaccustomed to the rigors of marching and movement, were thrust onto the roads leading south and west from Petersburg and Richmond.

For a solid week, the opposing armies in Virginia marched and fought, moving every day. It was constant, and it was grueling. Between April 2 and April 8, the armies covered 100 miles, moving across the muddy roads of central Virginia in a week of scattered showers. In the rapidly unfolding sequence of events, Confederate and Union troops each managed to obtain numerical superiority or surprise attacks during the week-long retreat at different times.

TOP: Appointed commander of all Confederate armies, Lee attempted to coordinate his movements with those of General Joseph E. Johnston in North Carolina. (si) BOTTOM: Commander of all Union armies, Ulysses S. Grant was 42 years old when he met with Lee at the McLean House. (loc)

It was a chaotic and hectic effort—suddenly moving the army and its entire support system from its ensconced positions. Sailors and marines marched as infantry, abandoning their heavy guns and ships. The government had also evacuated, with President Jefferson Davis, the cabinet, the Confederate treasury, and various clerks and bureaucrats rumbling south of Richmond on a train bound for Danville.

The immediate objective for Lee and the Army of Northern Virginia was Amelia Court House, about 40 miles southwest of Richmond. The larger strategy was for Lee to link up with the other main Confederate army, the Army of Tennessee commanded by Lt. Gen. Joseph E. Johnston, near Smithfield, North Carolina. Telegrams flashed between the two commanders, and they initiated plans to link their armies.

The first challenge was getting the entrenched army withdrawn from the Richmond and Petersburg defenses and then concentrating the scattered commands. At Amelia Court House, there were supposed to be supplies of food waiting. Yet upon arriving on the morning of April 4, there was none to be had.

Much of the industrial and business districts of Richmond were destroyed in the "Evacuation Fire." These are the ruins of the Richmond & Danville Railroad Station in Richmond. (loc)

Lee decided to pause and search the region for supplies. Around the small village, thousands of Confederate soldiers, cavalry, and wagons deployed and camped. "The failure to issue rations at Amelia Courthouse, as expected, left us for thirty-six hours without a mouthful to eat," Pvt. A. C. Jones of the 3rd Arkansas noted.

In the meantime, Union troops closed in on them from two directions. Lee had to keep the army moving.

From Amelia Court House, the Confederates retreated south, pursued by the Union army. Fast-moving troops of Maj. Gen. Phillip Sheridan's cavalry and the V Corps got there first, followed by the II and VI Corps, blocking Lee's direct route at the small town of Jetersville. "I never saw Gen. Lee seem so anxious to bring on a battle in my life as he seemed this afternoon," observed Gen. Edward P. Alexander, "but a conference with Gen. W. H. F. Lee in command of the cavalry in our front seemed to disappoint him greatly."

Lee had intended to move south into North Carolina, but Sheridan now forced him west, forever altering the campaign. Had Lee attacked to force his way, there potentially could have been a large battle, and perhaps a negotiated surrender, at Jertersville.

Lee's army turned west, with its command structure shattered, its hopes of reinforcement gone, and its hope of resupply slipping away. Skirmishing continued daily as the Union army doggedly pursued.

The constant marching and combat was exhausting. Private Carlton McCarthy of Cutshaw's Battery recalled, "the march was almost continuous, day and night, and it is with the greatest difficulty that a private in the ranks can recall with accuracy the dates and places on the march. Night was day—day was night. There was no . . . time to sleep, eat, or rest, and the events of morning became strangely intermingled with the events of evening."

Virginia artilleryman Percy Hawes agreed: "[T]urning night into day renders it almost impossible for me to separate the days. During the next day or two our lives were simply those of marching and fighting and fighting and marching. If we halted at all, it was to fight. There was scarcely an hour in the day that our line was not harassed."

Commanding the Army of the Shenandoah, Maj. Gen. Phil Sheridan's troopers and scouts played a vital role in trapping the Confederate army. (na)

Sergeant Llewellyn Shaver of the 60th Alabama noted, "Along the route were thickly strewn, evidence of the desperate and disastrous character of the movement—dead and dying animals—burning wagons—abandoned muskets, cannons, caissons, ordnance trains, knapsacks, blankets, and camp-equipage of every description—and saddest of all, exhausted and straggling men."

Union soldiers were pushed, too. "It was now a question of legs and endurance," wrote Capt. Albert Maxfield of the 11th Maine. "On and on our men plodded." Another from Illinois stated that they were "days without stopping for meals or sleep."

April 6 found the armies in western Amelia County. It was a momentous day in the campaign and illustrates the various moving parts ongoing simultaneously. Lee's immediate goal was Farmville, where he hoped to rest his exhausted men and receive supplies at the town's rail yard. Union forces were in close pursuit.

Major General Edward Ord, commanding the Army of the James, dispatched Union troops on a dangerous mission well ahead of the rest of the army: destroy the river crossing at High Bridge, about four miles from Farmville. This was an enormous railroad bridge over the Appomattox River. Had they succeeded, they would have prevented a large part of Lee's army from escaping.

Confederate cavalry arrived in time to defend the bridge, however, and attack the two infantry regiments. Outnumbered and overwhelmed, the Federals fell back, although more than 800 of them were captured, including a brass band.

Yet later that same day, at Sailor's Creek, the

Maj. Gen. Edward Ord was one of Grant's most trusted subordinates. He aggressively pushed his men on one last forced march to reach Appomattox on April 9, and his infantry blunted the last attack of the Army of Northern Virginia. (na)

High Bridge is more than 2,400 feet long and 125 feet high, making it the longest recreational bridge in Virginia and among the longest in the United States. (VDCR)

Confederate army met a disaster of unprecedented magnitude. Strung out on parallel roads, the army was vulnerable, and troops of the Army of the Potomac and the Army of the Shenandoah attacked at three points. Units in the Confederate column had gotten separated, resulting in a gap. The Confederates tried to stop and fight, but were overwhelmed by the Federals.

Much of Lt. Gen. Richard Ewell's corps was captured, along with Ewell himself. In all, Lee lost one-fifth of his army in one day: 8,000 men, nine generals (including his son, Maj. Gen. Custis Lee), about 50 battle flags, and many cannons, wagons, horses, and supplies.

It was one of the worst defeats of the whole war, and Lee wondered out loud if his army had been dissolved.

The next day, April 7, Lt. Gen. Ulysses. S. Grant wrote a letter to Lee, calling on him to surrender. Grant pointed out that his army had lost many men at Sailor's Creek. Surely the time had come to end the fighting. Lee replied that he did not think his situation was that desperate, but asked Grant what terms he would offer. Grant replied that the Confederates would be allowed to go home if the army surrendered.

As the survivors from Sailor's Creek staggered into Farmville to reunite with the main army, Lee finally

An enduring image from Sailor's Creek came when artist Alfred Waud sketched the capture of Lee's Second Corps (top). The location where that event took place sits slightly to the northeast of the visitor center (bottom); in the photo, the visitor center sits just out of sight beyond the crest of the hill. (loc)(cm)

realized things had reached a crisis level. There was little time to rest, and Lee decided to cross the Appomattox River and continue west on the north side of the river. The next objective was Campbell Court House (now Rustburg), with the ultimate goal of reaching Johnston in North Carolina.

In taking the road north of the river, however, the Army of Northern Virginia was on a longer road to the west, and if the Federals moved fast enough to the south, they could block the road. Lee felt it was worth the risk: the bulk of the Union army still had to cross the Appomattox River, and he hoped to distance himself in the meantime.

However, later that day—still April 7—the Confederates took up a position around Cumberland Church, north of Farmville, to face the Union troops who had crossed the river at High Bridge. At the battle of Cumberland Church, the Union II Corps assaulted a hastily built defensive line. In the combat, the 5th New Hampshire lost its flag and several men. The next day, however, the colors and the men were retaken in the wake of the Confederate retreat. This was the last Union battle flag taken by the Army of Northern Virginia in combat.

On April 8, the Southern army continued on the muddy roads to the west, pursued by the II and VI Corps. To the south of the Appomattox River, the Army of the James and the V Corps moved in a parallel direction.

Espionage was important in the campaign. Sheridan, for instance, used a group of men known as Jesse Scouts or Young's Scouts. They wore Confederate uniforms, spoke with Southern accents, and knew enough about Lee's army to blend in, being familiar with commanders and units. They wreaked havoc that week, capturing a Confederate general, spreading false reports, setting up ambushes, redirecting lines of march, and gathering intelligence. Soon they set the stage for the capture of Lee's entire army.

One of Sheridan's scouts, riding ahead, met Confederate supply trains and instructed the engineer to move ahead to Appomattox Station. Word went back to

Lee was making for Appomattox Station, which offered the hope of both resupply and escape. A brief but furious evening battle broke out there the night before the surrender. Nothing remains of the historic station today, but tracks still run through downtown Appomattox. (loc)

Sheridan, who dispatched Maj. Gen. George Custer's division to advance and capture them. The action sealed the Confederates' fate.

The two commanding generals continued to exchange letters, each feeling the other out. Grant's first letter of April 7 calling on Lee to surrender had met with a firm negative reply, but Lee did state his desire to "avoid useless effusion of blood," thus keeping the door open for further negotiations. He followed up by asking what terms Grant might offer. The Federal commander received Lee's reply early on the morning of April 8.

Grant replied that the Confederates would be "disqualified for taking up arms again against the Government of the United States until properly exchanged." In other words, they would be free to go home and not sent to prison or otherwise punished.

This reply reached Lee that evening as fighting erupted at Appomattox Station. Lee wrote back that he did not intend to surrender the army, but wanted to know how the two sides could achieve "the restoration of peace." In other words, Lee hoped to end the fighting, but not surrender. In closing, he emphasized his willingness to meet the next morning to discuss peace, but not surrender.

This message reached Grant late on April 8, and he began to compose an answer. His reply, sent on the morning of April 9, stated that he lacked the authority to discuss peace—meaning political settlement—but explained that the quickest way to peace was for the army to lay down its arms.

Earlier that year Lincoln had advised Grant that he wanted to end the war quickly and hoped that his general would find ways to ease the pain and tension of the war. Not privy to this, the Confederates feared Grant because of the nickname he'd brought from Fort Donelson and reinforced at Vicksburg as "Unconditional Surrender."

Before further correspondence took place, military events intervened.

Along Lee's Retreat Route

Lee's retreat route is well-marked by a series of more than twenty-five wayside markers, beginning at Pamplin Historical Park outside Petersburg and continuing on in such places as Sutherland, Namozine Church, Amelia Springs, Rice's Depot, High Bridge, Farmville, Cumberland Church, High Bridge, and Burkeville. Short-range radio messages broadcast at most of the stops (transcripts are available online at www.civilwartraveler.com).

Along the way, visitors can hike along the 31-mile High Bridge Trail or they can stop at Sayler's Creek Battlefield State Park. The park, which consists of 370 acres, has a visitor center with exhibits and an orientation program. Several original structures remain on the battlefield: the Hillsman house, the Lockett house, and the Christian house.

To visit these points of interest:

Visitors can follow the movements of the armies using the Lee's Retreat Driving Tour. Created in the 1990s, the success of this unique driving tour has led to a proliferation of Civil War Trails across Virginia and in other states. (cm)

Pamplin Historical Park
6125 Boydton Plank Road
Petersburg, VA

High Bridge Trail State Park *(closest to the bridge)*
River Road (three miles off N. Main St.)
Farmville, VA

Sailor's Creek Battlefield State Park
6541 Saylers Creek Road
Rice, VA

The Confederacy's Black Troops

The only combat by black Confederate troops occurred during Lee's retreat on April 5 at Painesville, a small town in western Amelia County.

On March 23, the Confederate Congress had allowed the recruitment of blacks for military service, an unpopular decision but one supported by Lee. Both free African Americans who volunteered as well as slaves offered by their owners could join. Recruiting began across the Confederacy in March and continued until interrupted by the war's end.

There has been a great deal written about—and speculated about— the makeup and motivations of these men. We can perhaps say that some may have legitimately believed in the Confederate cause, while some simply saw an opportunity to escape from slavery, much as others had done during the American Revolution when various states offered freedom to slaves who served.

The unit of black soldiers that formed in Richmond attracted much attention. "[T]he knowledge of the military art they already exhibit was something remarkable," the *Richmond Daily Examiner* noted. "They moved with evident pride and satisfaction to themselves."

The unit left the capital, joining the army on the retreat, assigned to guard wagons. During the westward flight, the Confederate army used several parallel roads for its wagon trains to allow the army to move efficiently and not clog the main roads. At Painesville on April 5, however, Union cavalry caught up with part of the wagon train near Flat Creek.

The cavalry swept in and were met with a volley by the black troops. After regrouping, the horsemen charged again and overran the black Confederates. A North Carolina battery deployed to help, but it was too little, too late.

"I saw a wagon train guarded by Confederate negro soldiers . . ." a white Southern soldier recalled. "When within about one hundred yards of an in the rear of the wagon train, I observed some Union cavalry a short distance away on elevated ground forming to charge and the negro soldiers forming to meet the attack, which was met successfully. . . . The cavalry charged again, and the negro troops surrendered."

Many Union troops and officers wrote of seeing blacks among Confederate prisoners, though this was not necessarily new, as slaves and servants had been taken in

battles during the whole war. At Painesville, some of the black troops were "highly delighted" in being taken and spared further combat.

Little is known of the composition, size, and organization of these units, nor their unit designation. Because they were still being formed and recruited so close to the war's end, they saw little action. It seems that only companies were organized; there was no chance to create regiments and brigades, as was planned. Had the war continued another month, though, the full-scale deployment and engagement of Confederate black troops would have been a reality.

The efforts of black soldiers in the Union army has long been acknowledged by historians; unfortunately, few details exist regarding the limited service blacks performed with the Confederate army. (loc)

The Last Charge

CHAPTER TWO

On April 8, the Army of Northern Virginia reached Appomattox Court House. The reserve artillery, moving ahead of the army, passed through the town at midday and moved on two miles to Appomattox Station. Late in the afternoon the infantry followed, and the army camped that night just east of the village. Days of rain and cool weather had made them—and their Federal counterparts—miserable.

Appomattox Court House was a village of little more than 120 residents; nearly half were slaves. The town had the courthouse, a tavern, lawyers' offices, some stores, and a post office. Several roads converged here, and it came to life every month during court days, when people from all over the county came to conduct business.

Anxious civilians watched from doorways and windows as thousands of men, horses, and wagons passed by. Many others fled or hid in their homes. The only civilian killed during the subsequent battle of Appomattox Court House was a slave, Hannah Reynolds.

The army that arrived at the village was weak, but not beaten in spirit. The men in the ranks knew their situation was desperate, but they had been in tight spots before. "Up to this time there was not a man in the command who had the slightest doubt that General Lee would be able to bring his army safely out of its desperate straits . . ." Pvt. A. C. Jones of the 3rd Arkansas recalled.

Yet the army's organization was in chaos. The army that arrived at Appomattox was an ad-hoc organization that reflected the chaos of the preceding week. Events moved so quickly that captured or wounded officers could

The North Carolina monument marks the last battle position of the troops on the morning of April 9, when the order to withdraw was received. (cm)

Maj. Gen. George A. Custer built his Civil War career on aggressive—and effective— use of his cavalry. On April 8, they helped seal off the Army of Northern Virginia's escape route at Appomattox Station. (na)

not be properly replaced; commands were merged due to high attrition or lack of leaders. Cavalry brigades were combined, but their commanders were not recorded in the official records. Such poor record-keeping makes it difficult for modern historians to accurately reconstruct the army's command structure and order of battle; many commanders and unit compositions are simply unknown and never will be.

Many local men from Appomattox County were in the approaching Confederate army—members of the 2nd Virginia Cavalry and the 18th and 46th Virginia Infantry. Some men even crossed their own farms or passed by their homes over those few days.

Not to be confused with the village of Appomattox Court House, Appomattox Station was a small railroad stop where Lee's army was hoping to obtain food. Railroads had been important all along: it was the network of railroads that brought supplies into Petersburg and kept Lee's army fed and supplied. Once the retreat began, Lee moved towards railroad depots for supplies along the march.

On the evening of April 8, Union cavalry under Maj. Gen. George A. Custer captured three trains at Appomattox Station loaded with rations, clothing, ammunition, and blankets that were waiting for the Confederates. Beyond the trains at the station sat the Confederate reserve artillery, and Custer quickly ordered his troopers to charge against them.

Much of the battle was fought after sunset in the growing darkness. The Confederate artillery fired as the Union cavalry charged. "It was too dark to see anything," one soldier wrote, adding that "the flashing and the roaring and the shouting" sounded "as if the devil himself had just come up."

Colonel Alanson Randol wrote that "six bright lights suddenly flashed directly before us. A tornado of canister-shot swept over our heads, and the next instant we were in the battery."

After three charges, the Union cavalry captured 25 Confederate cannons—one-fourth of the army's reserve artillery. The rest were dispersed and unavailable for further use.

Not only did the Federals capture the trains and cannons, but the cavalry also blocked the road, cutting off Lee's retreat. Custer's actions sealed the Army of Northern Virginia's fate.

*   *   *

After the action at Appomattox Station, another force of Union cavalry went forward into the darkness. Led by Col. Augustus Root, the 15th New York Cavalry and elements of the 2nd New York Cavalry charged into the village, where sleeping Confederates and supply wagons lined the road.

A brief firefight ensued along the Stage Road, and many saddles were emptied. Root fell, mortally wounded, and the troopers retreated back out of the village. Reinforcements joined them, including a two-gun battery of artillery. They deployed along the stagecoach road on a hill overlooking the village. Making a hasty defensive line of fence rails, they settled down for the night, carbines at the ready.

Among the Confederates killed in this evening encounter in the village was Pvt. Jesse Hutchins of the 5th Alabama Battalion. He enlisted on April 15, 1861, in Livingston, Alabama, and had survived four years of war, only to die in the final few hours.

Half a mile to the west at Lee's headquarters, Lt. Col. Charles Marshall recalled, "We lay upon the ground, near the road, with our saddles for pillows, our horses . . . eating the bark from the trees for want of better provender, and with our faces covered with the capes of our overcoats to keep out the night air."

The officers and men ate what little rations they had. "Somebody had a little corn meal, and somebody else had a tin can, such as is used to hold hot water for shaving," Marshall recounted. "A fire was kindled, and each man in his turn, according to rank and seniority, made a can of

Many of Col. Augustus Root's personal effects are now on display at the Appomattox Court House visitor center. (dd)

Lee's council of war: Lt. Gen. James Longstreet (left), Lt. Gen. John Brown Gordon (center), and Maj. Gen. Fitzhugh Lee (right). (loc)(loc)(loc)

The face of Lee's leadership team looked far different on the night of April 8 than it had earlier in the war. From left: John Gordon of Georgia led the last attack launched by the Army of Northern Virginia; he would later lead the troops in the surrender ceremony on April 12. The troops of James Longstreet, one of Lee's most trusted subordinates, held off the Army of the Potomac at the rear of the army's retreat. Gen. Fitzhugh Lee, nephew of the army commander, led the remnants of the Confederate cavalry. Lee met with them at a spot still marked in the woods, near the Stage Road. (achnhp)

corn-meal gruel, and was allowed to keep the can until the gruel became cool enough to drink. General Lee, who reposed as we had done, not far from us, did not . . . have even such a refreshment as I have described."

At ten o'clock on April 8, Lee and his exhausted officers held a council of war at his headquarters along the stagecoach road. Here it was acknowledged that Union cavalry was in front of them, and the officers agreed on an attack to break through and continue the retreat.

*   *   *

The final battle between the major field armies in Virginia began early on April 9.

Lieutenant General John Gordon's II Corps moved through the village to the western side at about two o'clock in the morning. His divisions were deployed, right to left, as follows: Brig. Gen. William Wallace's, Maj. Gen. Bryan Grimes', Brig. Gen. James Walker's, and Brig. Gen. Clement Evans'. With supporting cavalry from Fitz Lee's Cavalry Corps, about 9,000 men awaited the dawn. Artillery was deployed in the village to support the attack. Some of the men in the ranks did not have weapons, having lost them in the week-long retreat.

As Capt. W. T. Jenkins of the 14th North Carolina looked around him, he took in the scene and reflected on the soon "to-be-historic place."

Bryan Grimes had his North Carolina infantry on the line early and waited for orders from Gordon. Fitz Lee

The Peers House sits at the eastern end of Appomattox village. From here, Confederate artillery fired the last shots of the Army of Northern Virginia. (cm)

and Gordon rode up a little later and began to discuss the order of attack. Gordon thought the enemy in front was cavalry, thus Fitz Lee's cavalry should lead the . . . attack. Fitz Lee argued there was mostly infantry at their front, consequently Gordon's infantry should lead off. Grimes got impatient with the discussion, probably because it was apparent that neither Gordon nor Fitz Lee wanted to order their men into what the two generals believed would be the last battle for the Army of Northern Virginia.

At about 7:30, the battle flags of the Army of Northern Virginia advanced in combat one last time on the fog-shrouded morning.

The attack got underway as Brig. Gen. William P. Robert's cavalry charged over the rolling ground toward Brig. Gen. Charles H. Smith's brigade of dismounted cavalry. Two of Smith's regiments had seven-shot Spencer carbines and 16-shot Henry rifles, and could hold out against larger numbers for a short time, but as the Confederate infantry came on, they fell back. "Across the field we dashed right up the guns, shooting the gunners and support down with our Colt's navies [pistols]," said Confederate Cavalryman John Bouldin.

The last gun captured by the Army of Northern Virginia fell into Confederate hands on the ridge overlooking the village.

The outnumbered Federals gave ground slowly, though, delaying long enough for the infantry of the XXIV and XXV Corps from the Army of the James to arrive. "They had reached this point at daylight after an all night march . . . and were ready for the business of the day," said Col. Richard Staats of the 6th Ohio Cavalry, noting the arrival of the colored troops, "and the way they looked, and the manner in which they went in at the word of command, was the most inspiring sight I had seen during nearly four years."

Sergeant Edward Tobie of the 1st Maine Cavalry recalled the feeling of relief at seeing the black and white

Several flags of truce were sent out in different directions to stop the fighting. (loc)

Union infantry arrive. As he saw them form up alongside the white infantry, he wrote that they were "black and white— side by side—a regular checker-board."

By about 10 o'clock, the massive Union line was advancing confidently, with the Army of the James coming from the west, joined by the V Corps on the south. Gordon now faced the combined might of more than double his own strength.

To the south, along LeGrand Road, Custer's division of cavalry also moved into position. As he rode along the battle line that morning, he was accompanied by a group of aides and orderlies who carried about 40 recently captured Confederate flags.

Gordon reported back to Lee that he could not hold out. The Army of Northern Virginia was surrounded, with the Army of the Potomac behind it and elements of the Army of the Shenandoah and the Army of the James in front.

Lee sent out a flag of truce around 10:30, with a note to Grant asking for a surrender meeting.

Several flags were sent out in different directions. One flag of truce was a white towel that a Confederate soldier had just purchased a few days before.

Eventually, the news spread that Lee and Grant were to meet. The armies stopped in place and ceased firing. Soldiers recalled that it was strange: the battlefield was suddenly quiet.

Captain Wilson T. Jenkins of the 14th North Carolina recalled that he and about 25 men took shelter around some buildings to make a stand, while the rest of the troops withdrew. They then saw a rider with a flag of truce pass by.

Because the Confederate attack had been initially successful, orders to cease firing were met with disbelief by some men. "When we halted," one Southern soldier noted, "we were surprised to notice that the firing had all ceased and to see that our line was marching back towards the court house, while the enemy were marching back from whence they came. A staff officer now rode up with orders for us to return to the court house also."

Near Trent's Farm Lane, Brig. Gen. William Cox's North Carolina brigade made a last stand. Facing west, his roughly 600 men would have stood in awe as 8,500 men from the Army of the James poured out of the woods less than a mile away. Across the field from the North Carolinians, Union regiments moved into position, flags fluttering above their lines.

Many soldiers knew the end was near, and several wrote about not wanting to be killed in the last hours of the war. However, about 700 men on both sides were killed and wounded in this last battle.

Lieutenant General James Longstreet ordered his artillery to form a line in the Appomattox River valley for Gordon to fall behind. "I accordingly selected a line about a thousand yards on our side of the village of Appomattox," Gen. E. P. Alexander recalled, "and put about five thousand infantry of . . . Mahone's, and Wilcox's divisions in position upon it, and crammed it full of artillery, making the last line of battle ever formed by the Army of Northern Virginia."

On the route into Appomattox Court House, a lone cannon sits beside the road. A nearby marker explains: "The last Federal battery taken by the Confederates was captured by the North Carolina cavalry brigade of Brig. Gen. W. P. Roberts at this place." (cm)(cm)

Mr. McLean's Parlor

CHAPTER THREE

APRIL 9, 1865

As the morning ticked by, Lee waited under an apple tree near the Appomattox River for a response from Grant. It came delivered by Lt. Col. Orville Babcock and Lt. William Dunn at about noon. The generals agreed that the meeting would take place in the village as soon as everyone could arrive.

Lee sent Pvt. Joshua Johns and aide Col. Charles Marshall into the town to find a place to meet. Marshall met a civilian named Wilmer McLean and asked for his help in finding a place to convene.

It was Sunday, and the courthouse was closed. McLean then showed Marshall an unfurnished building, which was not suitable. Finally, McLean took him to his own house, and Marshall thought it would suffice.

*   *   *

While the flags of truce were spreading out along the lines, one Union general rode up to the Confederates and demanded that they surrender unconditionally. He was taken to Longstreet, who refused, knowing that the Union officer had no authority to make the demand. He also knew that Lee and Grant were set to meet.

The Federal general said Longstreet would be responsible for any bloodshed, to which Longstreet replied that he could "go ahead and have all the bloodshed he wanted." Dejected, the officer rode away, his long blond hair flowing behind him. General Custer would have to be satisfied with the role he had already played in the campaign.

Lee, Grant, and their staffs entered the McLean house through these doors. Following the meeting, Grant and his staff stood on this porch and saluted Lee as he departed. The structure has been reconstructed since April 1865. (cm)

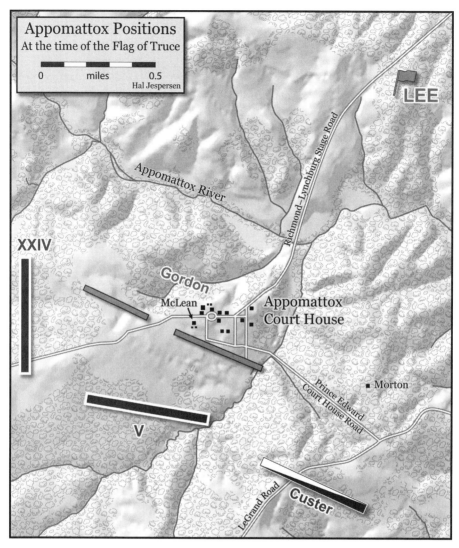

APPOMATTOX POSITIONS AT THE TIME OF THE FLAG OF TRUCE—The fighting ended around 10:30 a.m. on April 9. This map shows the final troop positions. Grant's headquarters was farther west along the stage road. Roughly seven hundred men from both armies were killed, wounded, or missing from the last battle.

*   *   *

Soon after the cease-fire, officers of the two sides met informally near the courthouse. The reunion included generals who were fellow West Pointers and Mexican War veterans. A bottle of brandy added to the atmosphere.

At about one o'clock, General Lee, wearing a new uniform and his sword, arrived at the McLean house

This photo of the McLean house was taken in 1865. The parlor where the generals met is to the left of the door. (loc)

and sat down at a table in the parlor to wait for General Grant. The McLean family—Wilmer and his wife, Virginia, and their five children—stayed out of the way when the officers arrived.

About half an hour later, Grant rode up, having come more than 20 miles by horseback. Grant did not want to keep Lee waiting and, besides, he had outpaced his baggage wagons. Therefore, there was no chance to change clothes. Thus he arrived in mud-spattered clothing, as did his whole staff.

Grant entered the room, and came face to face with General Lee. The two men had not seen each other in nearly 20 years.

They could not have been more different, Grant and Lee. The Union general was dirty, dressed in a plain uniform and lacking a sword. He was the son of a leatherworker from Illinois and had often struggled financially. General Lee was dressed in a new uniform, with a formal sword. He came from a wealthy Virginia family and was connected to some of the most powerful families in the state. Lee was 16 years older than Grant.

Despite their differences, and the different sides they fought for, they each had a common purpose: to end the fighting.

Those present included Lee and Marshall—the only two Confederates—as well as Grant; Gens. Phil Sheridan, Edward Ord, Seth Williams, John Rawlins, Michael Morgan, George Sharpe, and Rufus Ingles; Capt. Robert T. Lincoln (son of the president), and Lt. Cols. Orville Babcock, Adam Badeau, Ely Parker, Theodore Bowers, and Horace Porter.

The "legend of Wilmer McLean" has grown large in the century and a half since the Civil War. In 1861, McLean had lived outside the town of Manassas, and the battle of First Manassas erupted in his front yard. By 1865, worried that the tumult of war was upsetting his business as a sugar speculator, he had moved well away from the front to quiet Appomattox— where the war again found him. Thereafter, he reportedly liked to say, "The war started in my front yard and ended in my front parlor." (nps)

Reproductions of the chairs used by Lee (left) and Grant (right) sit in the parlor in the McLean house. The park has also reproduced the historic carpet pattern that was in the room. (dd)

The original table used by Grant, and the chairs used by both generals, sit in the Smithsonian's Museum of American History. Grant's chair is to the left, Lee's to the right. (cm)

Grant and Lee began by talking informally about the Mexican War, where they had both served. Lee soon suggested that they get down to business.

Historians today know surprising little from an important meeting that lasted an hour and a half and had more than a dozen witnesses. Several accounts exist, but not all agree on the details. They disagree on the order of events as well as the dialogue.

It seems clear that Lee asked what Grant's terms would be. Grant replied that the Confederates would have to surrender their arms and equipment, but would then be allowed to go home. Lee asked for this in writing, and Grant wrote out the terms and passed them to Lee.

Lee agreed, asking also that his men be allowed to keep their horses. Grant understood—spring planting time was at hand—and had his aide, Ely Parker, write up the terms. Parker had to borrow ink from Charles Marshall. Parker was a Seneca Indian and had been a friend of Grant for several years. Later, when Lee was introduced to Parker, Lee said he was glad to see one true American in the room. "We are all Americans," Parker replied.

After agreeing on the terms, Lee said that he had about 1,000 Union prisoners and no food for them, prompting Grant to ask how many men Lee had. Lee replied that because of recent losses, he did not know. Grant offered to send 25,000 rations over to the Confederates, which Lee felt would be sufficient.

Lee and Grant both left to return to their armies. Each had a lot to do. In the meantime, Union officers bought some of the furniture that was in Wilmer McLean's parlor, paying him for the tables and chairs that were used by the generals. One soldier even took a doll that had been in the room; it belonged to seven-year-old Lula, Wilmer McLean's daughter.

Captain Horner A. Plimpton of the 39th Illinois, looked down at the village from the ridge above. "I saw Gen. Lee when he took his leave of Gen. Grant after all the papers were signed," Plimpton wrote. "I watched the countenance of our gallant chieftain as he came away, it was beaming with smiles as he raised his hat when passing one of our sentinels who presented the proper salute . . ."

The news was a huge blow to the men of the Army of Northern Virginia. Private A. C. Jones of the 3rd Arkansas wrote, "When the news came, notwithstanding I had been partially prepared, to me it was a mental shock that I am unable to describe, just as if the world had suddenly come to an end." Captain Henry Chambers of the 49th North Carolina agreed, saying, "Can it be? Can it be? That after so noble a struggle, after so many deeds of heroism and valour, after the shedding of so much precious blood, after so much sorrow and suffering, borne, too, with such Spartan fortitude, can it be that after all this, we are to be subjugated!"

Some men talked of sneaking away to fight with the Army of Tennessee in North Carolina. More desperate were those who talked of leaving the country altogether, or journeying to Mexico to fight there. Others destroyed their rifles or hid their flags, so as not to surrender them. "We had torn our regimental flag from its staff and divided it into small pieces for each man to keep as a sacred relic," admitted Pvt. I. G. Bradwell of the 31st Georgia.

For most southerners, it was a shock: they went suddenly from soldiers to civilians. Fighting had gone on to literally the last moment. "[A]ll was confusion and uncertainty, and none could tell just what he future had in store for us," said Pvt. Thomas Devereux of the 6th Alabama.

As Robert E. Lee departed the McLean House, a Pennsylvania Brass Band struck up "Aud Lang Syne." (loc)

Left: Ely Parker was a long-serving member of Grant's staff, having been with him in the west. Because of his excellent penmanship, he was asked to write out the final terms. Right: The only other Confederate in the room was Lee's aide, Charles Marshall. (loc)(cphcw)

There were other adjustments to make, too. For years, the Confederates had lived a strict life of routine: drill, rations, receiving orders. Now they did not have to get up, eat, or stand guard. An artilleryman from the Bedford Light Artillery noted that on the next day, "we slept as late as we pleased." However, it was damp and cool during those April days, and Confederate Samuel H. Gray recalled, "The ground was as cold as a stone, and I awoke after a disturbed sleep stiff and sore in every joint."

The soldiers of both armies enjoyed the rest, though, and many remarked on the relief after such a trying week. "I have talked with some of them and find that they are as glad as we are that the war is over," said Pvt. Elijah H. Rhodes of the 2nd Rhode Island. "It seemed queer to sleep last night without fearing an attack."

Curious Union soldiers visited the Confederates, and many of them shared their meager rations, the Union army having outpaced its own supply lines. Said one South Carolinian, "It doesn't seem right to see them pass without hearing the click of a gun."

For the most part, there was respect shown by both sides. Captain John Robertson of the 23rd South Carolina noted that, "Never in all history was a captured army treated with so much respect. We were half starved, faint, and weary. We were given one day's short rations while there, the Federals stating that they themselves had very little food."

At the same time, one of the most enduring Appomattox legends took root, that of the apple tree. Confederate troops saw Lee, Marshall, Babcock, and Dunn assemble near an apple tree near the river crossing, just in front of the last line of battle. Unable to make out the features of the Union officer speaking with

Lee, many witnesses assumed it was Grant and that the surrender meeting took place there. By the end of the day, Union souvenir hunters chopped up the tree, even digging up its roots. Pieces of the apple tree (or more likely, of several area apple trees) were bought, sold, and traded all across the country, marketed as coming from the site where Lee surrendered to Grant.

Souvenir hunters frantically cut up the apple tree where Lee waited for Grant's message, mistakenly thinking the surrender took place here. Even the roots were dug up, and for decades slices of the apple tree were prized possessions. Today, a marker sits along the old State Road noting the site of the apple tree. It is seldom visited by park visitors. (loc)(dd)

On the Stage Road

CHAPTER FOUR

APRIL 10, 1865

The name of the village was Appomattox Court House, which is sometimes misleading to visitors today because nothing actually occurred in the courthouse itself during the surrender. Today, the park's visitor center and museum are in the building. Along this road, Colonel Root led his ill-fated charge, and Confederate troops stacked their weapons. (dd)

The two commanding generals met again on the morning of April 10, coming together on horseback at the eastern edge of the village. Other officers were nearby, but could not hear the conversation. Several important things came out of this impromptu meeting.

Grant asked Lee for assistance in arranging the surrenders of the other Confederate armies, but Lee said he lacked the authority to do so. Next, Lee asked Grant for proof that his soldiers had surrendered, and Grant agreed to have paroles printed. Finally, Grant stated his intention for the personal property, such as horses, of the officers and men to be kept, and he issued orders for Confederates to receive transportation home on military railroads and steamships.

While Grant was generous in victory, he did insist on a formal surrender ceremony. To that end, the generals agreed that a commission, formed of three officers from each side, should meet to work out the details of the surrender. Union Gens. John Gibbon, Wesley Merritt, and Charles Griffin met with Confederate Gens. James Longstreet, John Gordon, and William Pendleton.

The commissioners first gathered in the Clover Hill Tavern, but as Gibbon noted, they found it a "bare and cheerless place and at my suggestion we adjourned to the room in the McLean house where Gens. Grant and Lee had held their conference." Thus the McLean's parlor was not only the site of Lee and Grant's meeting, but also where the commission drew up the formal proceedings of the surrender.

The lesser known and little-documented meeting between the two commanders took place on April 10 at the eastern edge of the village. Out of earshot from fellow officers, the two generals discussed the larger military situation, but their exact conversation is unknown. (cm)

Among other things, they stipulated that the Confederate infantry would march into the village and surrender their arms, that officers and men could keep their personal horses and property (including officers' swords), and that the surrender would apply to all Confederate troops within a 20 mile radius of Appomattox.

It was also agreed that the surrender would occur over the next three days: the cavalry that day, followed by the artillery on April 11, and the infantry last on April 12.

Most of the Confederate cavalry had actually gotten away during the fighting on the morning of April 9, and only 1,559 cavalrymen remained in the camp above the Appomattox River, commanded by Col. Alexander Haskell. General Ranald MacKenzie received orders to meet the Southern cavalry on the road north of the village, where he received their sabers, firearms, and accoutrements. Few details of the cavalry's surrender exist.

For the artillery, it was simply a matter of unhitching the guns from the horses and leaving them in the road just east of the village. In fact, the Confederate's animals were so worn and exhausted that the guns could not have been moved far anyway. Lee's army had been static for nine months while in Petersburg, and neither the men nor animals had been in any condition for active campaigning when the evacuation occurred on April 2.

Some Confederate artillery units managed to get away from Appomattox. Cut off and without support, they destroyed their carriages and buried the guns. (achnhp)

Troops from Brig. Gen. John Turner's Division of the XXIV Corps, and later Brig. Gen. Joseph Bartlett's Division of the V Corps, oversaw the artillery surrender. The Confederates surrendered 61 cannons; more were later found in their camps.

This reproduction press sits in the tavern, where Union soldiers printed paroles for the Confederates. (cm)

The largest part of the surrender, and by far the most symbolic, would be the stacking of arms set for the morning of April 12—ironically, four years to the day that the firing began on Fort Sumter.

In the meantime, Union soldiers set up printing presses in the Clover Hill Tavern and began churning out parole passes for the Confederate soldiers. They worked round the clock to crank out 28,231 paroles off portable printing presses. The paroles stated that the man carrying the pass had surrendered. If, on the way home, the Confederate was stopped by any Union soldiers, he could show his pass and not be harmed or made prisoner. The paroles could be used by the Confederates to draw rations from any Union supply station on their way. They could also be used to ride on Union army railroads and ships to get home—welcome news for those going to far places like Texas or Mississippi.

An example of the more than 28,000 paroles printed for the Confederate soldiers. (achnhp)

*   *   *

At five o'clock on the morning of April 12, Union soldiers from the First Division of the V Corps marched into the village and lined the sides of the stagecoach road. Soon they could hear the Confederates marching towards them.

As the Confederates came up, the Union officer in charge, Maj. Gen. Joshua Chamberlain, ordered his men to "shoulder arms"—a marching salute to their enemies.

Quickly, the Confederate commander, Lt. Gen. John Gordon, ordered his men to shoulder arms, returning the salute. It was incredible: Union and Confederate soldiers facing each other and honoring each other. Nothing like this would occur at any following surrender.

As the Confederates marched in, they stopped, faced front, stacked their rifles in the road, and hung their cartridge boxes with ammunition on them. Then they rolled up their battle flags and placed them there, probably the hardest thing for them to do. Many of those flags had been through dozens of battles and were symbols of pride for the men.

A soldier from the 155th Pennsylvania wrote of the process: The Confederate troops marched in, and their officers called out, "Halt! Close up! Front Face! Stack Arms! Unsling Cartridge boxes! Hang on Stacks! Right Face! Forward! Countermarch by Files Right, March!" He also noted that they took the rifles after each unit surrendered and piled them in the rear.

During the ceremony, some Union and Confederate regiments recognized each other and recalled battles where they had fought during the previous four years. Captain B. W. Smith of the Palmetto Sharpshooters (SC) recalled one exchange. The Federals in front of his command called out, "What regiment is that?"

"Palmetto Sharpshooters," came the reply.

"16th Michigan," replied the Union soldiers.

Smith then turned to his men and said, "Boys, do you remember the 27th of June, 1862? This is the regiment that fired on us in the hollow, and we captured their banner."

The process went on until about three o'clock. They did not stop for lunch, and besides, a Pennsylvanian noted, there was "not a cracker nor a bean" in the Union army. At the end of the day, "there was a pile of muskets shoulder high, which the army wagons soon hauled away."

For the most part the surrender went smoothly, and without incident, but a South Carolinian, reflecting the bitterness felt by many, said, "I wished them all 'in the bad place.'"

Lieutenant Abner R. Cox of the Palmetto Sharpshooters (SC) noted, "a large force of Yankee infantry was drawn up on either side of the road, with flags flying and officers and men in full uniform. We marched up one line, and our Regt. stacked arms in front of the 118th Pennsylvania. The men were very civil and

Brig. Gen. Joshua Lawrence Chamberlain has become one of the most romanticized Union officers of the war because of modern pop culture treatment of his actions on Little Round Top on July 2, 1863. A near-fatal wounding at Petersburg the following year added to his mystique, and the myth-building has been capped off with flourish by his service at Appomattox. Chamberlain, officer of the day for the stacking of arms, supervised the ceremony and ordered the Union soldiers to stand at attention and salute the Confederates. (na)

polite, said they had met us before, and hoped it would be a long time before they met us again."

J. R. Birdlebrough of the 185th New York wrote of an incident after the stacking. One soldier

> seeing a chance for some fun and not realizing what the result would be, went to a house near by and, getting a shovelful of coals and throwing them down in the hole, began throwing in some of the cartridges which had been . . . emptied upon the ground. This made a considerable diversion at the time, but shortly an officer made his appearance and put a stop to the proceedings. Just about that time a gust of wind carried a spark up the bank, and I an instant pandemonium broke loose. One-half of the cartridges took fire and the bullets flew thick as hailstones, mules stampeded, and men had to take shelter behind houses. When the officers came around . . . and inquired who did it, no one knew.

The Confederates marched back to their camp, unarmed, and instantly turned from soldiers to civilians.

*   *   *

After surrendering their weapons and receiving their paroles, the former Confederate soldiers began their long march home. In the days after the surrender, thousands of men lined the country roads of Appomattox County. Men from Texas, Arkansas, Mississippi, Louisiana, Missouri, Florida, Alabama, Maryland, North Carolina, Georgia, Tennessee, South Carolina, and Virginia began their trek home.

Most started out as units, but soon it was apparent

The symbolic "stacking of arms" ceremony took place along the Stage Road through the center of the village. Appomattox would be the only surrender that included such formal proceedings. (loc)

that in large clusters they could not successfully obtain food from farms they passed on the way, and the men split up into smaller groups. Once they got close to home, they began to break off to get to their farms and houses.

Some Confederate soldiers who had made it to Lynchburg received their paroles there, once it was occupied by Union troops in the weeks after Appomattox. Others came back to Appomattox to get paroles issued there.

On April 10, the survivors of the 2nd Virginia Cavalry disbanded in Lynchburg at the fairgrounds where, on May 11, 1861, they had organized.

In the Confederate camp at Appomattox were about 1,000 Union prisoners, many of them taken at High Bridge. These men were turned over to the Union army after the surrender agreement.

The question of who was the last soldier killed in battle at Appomattox has persisted ever since the guns went silent. Private William Montgomery of the 155th Pennsylvania is one candidate. Wounded by an artillery shell, he wrote his mother in Pittsburgh on April 16 that hoped to be released "in about 15 or 20 days," adding that he did not want her "to fret yourself sick about me." Yet he did not recover, and was buried at Poplar Grove National Cemetery in Petersburg.

However, with fighting going on in several places, it may be impossible to determine who was the last killed in combat. Many wounded lingered for weeks, and several died from wounds throughout the rest of April and into May.

Witnesses recorded that Wilmer McLean tried to capitalize on his notoriety from the surrender and his Manassas connection—the battle of First Manassas had opened in his front yard on July 21, 1861. McLean offered his autograph for a dollar. "I was told that he thus received quite a golden harvest," reported Col. Alanson Randol of the 2nd New York Cavalry.

Lee had his aide Charles Marshall composed a farewell address. Lee indicated a few changes, and the final version has become a classic piece of Civil War literature. Read by adjutants to the men before they departed, it states:

After four years of arduous service marked by unsurpassed courage and fortitude, the Army of Northern Virginia has been compelled to yield to overwhelming numbers and resources. I need not tell the survivors of so many hard fought battles, who have remained steadfast to the last, that I have consented to the result from no distrust of them. But feeling that valor and devotion could accomplish nothing that could compensate for the loss that must have attended the continuance of the contest, I have determined to avoid the useless sacrifice of those whose past services have endeared them to their country. By the terms of the agreement, offices and men can return to their homes and remain until exchanged. You will take with you the satisfaction that proceeds from the consciousness of duty faithfully performed, and I earnestly pray that a merciful God will extend to you his blessing and protection. With an unceasing admiration of your constancy and devotion to your Country, and a grateful remembrance of your kind and generous consideration for myself, I bid you an affectionate farewell.

General Grant also composed a farewell, but not until much later, after other surrenders had occurred. Sent out on June 2, it reads:

By your patriotic devotion to your country in the hour of danger and alarm. . . . You have maintained the supremacy of the Union and the Constitution, overthrown all armed opposition to the enforcement of the law, and of the proclamation forever abolishing slavery, the cause and pretext of the rebellion, and opened the way to the rightful authorities to restore order and inaugurate peace on a permanent and enduring basis on every foot of American soil.

Appomattox is unique among the various surrenders for several reasons. The armies were in contact, and the Union army could physically oversee the surrender proceedings. There was a final battle, fought the morning of the surrender. Paroles were printed on site and distributed directly to the Confederates (and the paroles were printed using a check pattern, unlike at the later surrenders). The surrender was also sudden and largely unexpected—neither side had time to mentally prepare for the end of fighting and the sudden transition to peacetime.

No other Confederate force was so worn down. The Army of Northern Virginia had been hounded for a week before succumbing. Of all the Confederate forces that surrendered, none were in worse shape—mentally, physically, and administratively.

Lastly, Appomattox set the tone for how the war

"I BID YOU AN AFFECTIONATE FAREWELL."

— *ROBERT E. LEE*

One of the few reminders of the last battle, the cemetery holds the remains of eighteen Confederate and one Union soldier. Resting here is Jesse Hutchins of the 5th Alabama Battalion, who enlisted in the spring of 1861, and survived four years of war, only to die in the final hours. (cm)

would end, with generous terms. The Union fed their former foes and assisted in getting them home. The other surrenders that followed included that spirit of generosity, but were more chaotic, confusing, and stressful.

President Lincoln received news of the surrender from Grant that very night, on April 9. Washington, D.C., erupted in celebration. The president spoke to a crowd at the White House, but his tone was somber and determined, not celebratory. Referencing the work ahead with Reconstruction, and the challenges that had arisen so far in Union-occupied Louisiana, he sounded a cautionary note: "Shall [we] sooner have the fowl by hatching the egg than by smashing it?"

Lincoln did not have long to enjoy the day's success. His assassination five days later plunged the country into depression and put many Northerners in a mood for revenge. This greatly affected the following surrenders, especially the next one in North Carolina.

At Appomattox Court House

Appomattox Court House became a national historical park in 1954, although preservation efforts date back as far as 1930. The park contains more than a dozen buildings, a museum, and a number of historical markers. Beyond the historic village, a four-mile hiking trail connects the parking area near the North Carolina monument to the west with Lee's Headquarters to the east.

Eighteen-year-old Lafayette Meeks, son of store owner Francis Meeks, enlisted with a local cavalry unit in 1861. He died of disease the following year and was buried behind the family store. The grave serves as a reminder that the town felt the impact of war long before the armies arrived. (cm)

The Raine monument in the Raine family cemetery was erected by C. Hunter Raine in memory of his father, Capt. Chas. J. Raine, a Confederate artillerist who was killed at Mine Run on Nov. 30, 1863. Members of the family are buried there. (cm)

Opened in 2012, Museum of the Confederacy—Appomattox was one of the largest projects of the entire Civil War Sesquicentennial. The museum features the uniform and sword Lee wore on April 9, as well as numerous battle flags surrendered at Appomattox. (dd)

THE LAST GRAND REVIEW

ON THIS SITE, APRIL, 1865, THE LAST GRAND
REVIEW OF THE CONFEDERATE ARMY WAS HELD.
THE TROOPS WERE REVIEWED BY GENERAL J. E.
JOHNSTON, GOVERNOR VANCE AND OTHERS.

ERECTED BY ELI OLIVE CAMP # 1460 SONS OF
CONFEDERATE VETERANS, APRIL 1990.

Retreat Through Raleigh

CHAPTER FIVE
APRIL 1865

One hundred miles to the south of Appomattox, the same rain storms that drizzled on the disintegrating Army of Northern Virginia battered troops in North Carolina—but the similarities end there. The closing of the war in North Carolina is not a neat, compact story like that at Appomattox. The armies did not perform a formal surrender ceremony. The commanders are less prominent. The procedures were not even carried out evenly: some units received paroles in the field, others not until they reached home. The armies were not even in contact. Events occurred at various, widespread locations and are not easy to follow. It was extremely chaotic.

Although Gens. William T. Sherman and Joseph E. Johnston negotiated at the Bennett place near Durham, the Confederate army's camps were spread over a wide area, with the troops hunkered down at High Point, New Salem, Jamestown, Salisbury, Trinity College, Bush Hill, and Greensboro. Union forces were more than 60 miles away in Raleigh. The stacking of arms and issuing of paroles—the only tangible motions of surrender—took place at the various Confederate campsites, for the most part, with no Union troops in sight.

For those who experienced it, the war's end at Greensboro was tedious, fraught with rumors, and agonizingly slow. Speculation abounded—rumors in the Confederate camps ranged from Grant surrendering to Lee, to Lee surrendering to Grant, to Johnston surrendering, to tales of both forces joining in a war with Mexico. The fighting was suspended, then resumed, then called off again.

It was simply maddening.

North Carolina governor Zeb Vance and other dignitaries turned out for the army's reviews in early April. (dd)

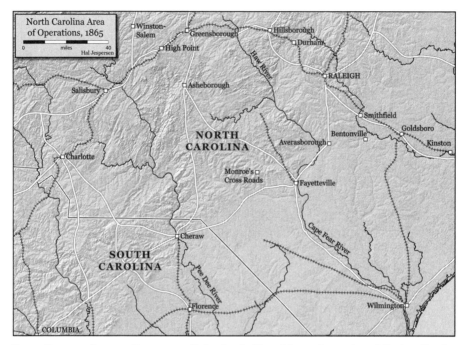

NORTH CAROLINA AREA OF OPERATIONS—Following battles at Avaresborough and Bentonville, the Confederate army fell back from Smithfield, through Raleigh, towards Greensboro. Sherman's Union forces were larger but somewhat bedraggled from living off the land, which made them potentially vulnerable. Johnston, unable to find an opening, kept his army out of Sherman's reach. Sherman had pursued as far as Raleigh when negotiatons began.

* * *

The soldiers of the Army of Tennessee received four pieces of dreadful news in April 1865—one after another—that broke their morale. First was the army's massive reorganization, followed by news of the fall of Richmond. Then came word of Lee's surrender, followed by news of their own surrender after four exhausting years.

Charged with organizing the defense of North Carolina against Sherman's Union forces, Johnston had a mix of troops from various Confederate departments, including remnants of the Army of Tennessee; troops transferred from the Army of Northern Virginia; units from the Department of South Carolina, Georgia, and Florida; and the North Carolina Reserves.

Johnston also had an overabundance of officers, many of whom had been shuffled about from various commands, and nearly all of whom harbored bitter feelings toward each other. The leadership core included Maj. Gen. Pierre Gustav Beauregard, who had served with Johnston at the war's first major battle at Manassas;

William T. Sherman (left) and Joseph E. Johnston (right) had squared off earlier in the war during the opening phases of the Atlanta campaign, where Sherman had admired Johnston's skill at defensive warfare. (loc)(loc)

Maj. Gen. Wade Hampton; Maj. Gen. Joseph Wheeler; Maj. Gen. Braxton Bragg, who once commanded the very army he was now a part of; and Maj. Gen. William Hardee, who had been detached from this army but whose independent command was now absorbed back into it. It was an odd, cumbersome, awkward situation.

However, the need to stop Sherman's march was urgent, and there was no time to integrate units and allow commanders to get familiar with their men. The army would fight with the disadvantage of never having worked together.

Their first battle that spring took place at Avarsboro near Fayetteville, from March 15-16. This action delayed, but did not stop, Sherman's progress.

Johnston then planned a major effort at Bentonville, taking advantage of a gap between the wings of Sherman's forces. Fighting raged here from March

The site of the largest battle in North Carolina, Bentonville represented Johnston's attempt to destroy a portion of Sherman's army and even the odds. (bd)

19-21. The Confederates came close to success, but Union troops held on with dogged determination.

Pulling back, both armies rested and prepared for the next step. First, Johnston took measures to improve his supply lines, working with officers to accumulate stores and improve rail service to the west and south. By the end of March, order had been imposed on the rail line running from Washington, Georgia, to Charlotte, North Carolina, and supplies were flowing to Johnston's men.

On April 9—the same day that Lee met with Grant in the McLean house at Appomattox Court House—

Johnston reorganized the army camped near Smithfield. He ordered that the massive project move "with all possible speed, Sherman will not give us much rest." In another order, he wrote that consolidation begin "without delay."

The army had seen consolidations before, but this was more drastic than anything experienced previously. The army had too many undersized regiments and an overabundance of general officers. Many regiments were combined into new "Consolidated" Regiments.

Most field armies had been reorganized over the course of the war, yet this was the most radical reorganization any of them had experienced. Breaking up and reconstituting infantry regiments and artillery batteries is quite different from reorganizing corps. For the common soldier it was a very personal and very powerful change.

"All the officers are now anxious about the consolidation which is to take place in a few days," wrote Pvt. William Dixon of the 1st Georgia, "as the most of us will be thrown out, the regiment not being more than large enough to make one company or two at the most. My company is now the largest in the regiment and it only numbers fourteen men and four officers."

Confederates passed through this area on their march toward Raleigh. (dd)

The Army of Tennessee reduced 30 batteries of artillery to 10. Eleven Arkansas regiments were consolidated into one, seven Florida regiments into one, eight Texas regiments into one, and 39 Tennessee regiments into four (each having nine or 12 of the old commands).

With the army reconstituted, Johnston pulled back towards Raleigh, ahead of Sherman's advance. News of Richmond's fall was a tremendous blow, and it put Johnston on the road to link up with Lee somewhere near the state line. However, rumors soon began to filter through the army about Lee's surrender. Disbelief turned to shock when confirmation arrived.

"[W]e met an old Confederate veteran [who said] our army in Virginia had now surrendered," Capt. William Calhoun of the 42nd Georgia wrote. "This statement was disbelieved, and our general commanding ordered his arrest. . . . [O]ther reports . . . seemed to confirm it. He was released in the morning with apology."

The Army of Tennessee retreated through Raleigh,

abandoning the capital without a fight, and continued marching west through Hillsborough and Chapel Hill towards Greensboro, a major supply and railroad center. Johnston knew that President Davis and the Cabinet were on the way from Danville and looked to meet with them to decide the future of the struggle.

As the Army of Tennessee arrived in the Greensboro area, it entered a region sharply divided by the war. Guilford, Randolph, and Davidson Counties were home to Quakers and Moravians, and many others who supported a large anti-war movement. The arrival of the massive army also strained resources for civilians.

One example of civil unrest is seen in a letter from Randolph County resident Martha Sheets to Governor Zeb Vance:

> *Dear Sur, I can tell you the truth but I dont reckon that you want to her hit. If you dont send me too bushels of wheat and too bushels and a peck of corn in the corse of tenn days I will send enuf of Deserters to mak you sufer that you never suffered before. And send me good grain if you want to live. Pepel tell me Whow mean you was before I went to see you But I found you wors than ther told me and athout a grate alterrashen you will go to the Devile and that soon. Ther you have got all of your suns at home and when my husband is gon and he has Dun Work for you and you try to Denie hit and When this ware Brake out you sad goe Boys, ill spend the Last doler for your famelys and Drat your ole sold you never have dun a thing for the pore Wiming yet, you nasty old Whelp. You have told lys to get your suns out of this War And you dont care for the rest that is gon nor for ther famekeys, now you ma depend if you dont Bring that grain to my dore you Will sufer and that Bad.*

*   *   *

Rain pounded central North Carolina. Rivers flooded, and the ground became saturated. Weary soldiers trudged through the muddy roads, pushing supply wagons and cannons.

The high waters of the Haw River in Alamance County posed a major obstacle for the army as it moved west from Raleigh. "The water was generally waist-deep, sometimes when on a rock not so deep, then deeper as the rock was stepped off," recalled an officer with Maj. Gen. Robert Hoke's Division. "It was rough wading."

Hoke's Division ended up crossing near Holt's

Little remains of the Confederate campsites in Greensboro to suggest the vast army that once occupied the grounds. (bd)

Mill. Lieutenant Janius C. Ellington of the 15th North Carolina wrote of the general's actions:

> *He moved the head of his column to this point, directed on man to seize his horse's tail, and another to grasp this man's shoulder, and another and another until he had a long line, swam his hose across the narrow stream and discharging his cargo safely on the opposite bank ,would quickly return for another. The rapidity with which the men were carried over was astonishing.*

One of the more colorful commanders in the Army of Tennessee, Frank Cheatham displayed great charisma on and off the battlefield. (loc)

Another general also tried to motivate his men without success. Major General Benjamin F. Cheatham, frustrated with the delay in crossing, expressed his displeasure to the soldiers standing along the flooded banks. They refused to cross and "emphasized their determination with some pretty lively swearing." Cheatham tried to force one man into the water, and the two ended up wrestling, falling to the ground, and rolling into the cold water. The regiment agreed to cross, but stopped when three wagons attempting the ford were swept away.

Colonel John W. Hinsdale of the 3rd North Carolina Junior Reserves wrote of "a bacon wagon and two wagons carrying guns" being lost in the crossing, along with several mules and even a few men. Another soldier wrote of "water up to their cartridge boxes."

Colonel Charles W. Broadfoot of the 1st North Carolina Junior Reserves noted, "many narrow escapes from drowning occurred, especially among the boys." Several wagons and artillery guns with the Junior Reserves were swept away in the current, though. At one point a young soldier went under, and a comrade pulled him out of the raging water. The youth dove in again, and was again rescued. After a third time, the irritated and drenched man asked the soldier why he was going down into the water. He replied, "My gun's down thar and I'm trying to git hit."

Composed of troops from 15 to 18 years old, the Junior Reserves were marching through or near their home counties, abandoning them to the enemy. This must have dampened their spirits even more.

Yet to his credit, Johnston kept his army out of Sherman's reach, and he made good strides to reorganize his supply and transport systems in his rear. In short, he had options that Lee did not, and at no time was he even close to being trapped.

As events unfolded more gradually in North Carolina, the common soldiers had time to think and reflect on their situation, unlike their comrades in Virginia, where actions moved at a dizzying pace. Many soldiers simply tried to make the best of their situation. Captain Samuel Foster of the 1st Texas Cavalry recalled:

> Soon after we arrive at our new camp today some of our men found two barrels of Old Apple brandy buried under the root of an old pine tree that had blown down. One barrel of it was brought to Our Brigade and taped- Every one helped themselves, and of course some get funny, some get tight some get gentlemanly drunk and some get dog drunk, of this latter class are all the officers from our Maj up. Kept up a noise nearly all night, but no one gets mad-all in good humor.

*   *   *

In the meantime, President Jefferson Davis and his Cabinet made their way south from Danville to Greensboro, narrowly escaping Union cavalry. In Greensboro, the party split their time between their railroad cars at the yard and the rented home of Naval Capt. John Taylor Wood. "Houses all closed," the captain recorded. "The people are afraid to take any one in; the Cabinet, General Cooper, and others are sleeping in the cars. The surrender of General Lee and his entire army is confirmed. I can hardly realize this overwhelming disaster, it crushes the hopes of nearly all."

Upon arriving in Greensboro, Johnston first went to Beauregard's headquarters, a railroad car near the one occupied by the president. An hour later, both officers were standing in front of Davis and the cabinet. The

Second in command under Johnston, Gen. P.G.T. Beauregard was efficient in organizing the defense of North Carolina. (loc)

meeting, intended to discuss strategy, was tense, no doubt made more so by the unpleasant surroundings.

Davis was undeterred in his conviction to continue the war, yet the generals insisted that the situation was hopeless. Some of the cabinet members agreed. Finally, a frustrated Davis agreed to allow Johnston to meet with Sherman to discuss a truce.

Outside, tensions built on the crowded streets of Greensboro. The town was filled with disorderly troops, escaped slaves, refugees, and deserters.

Several warehouses in the city bulged with food and supplies, tempting both soldiers and civilians alike. On April 15, a mob looted the warehouses. The crowd gathered on South Elm Street and first ransacked the Confederate Quartermaster Department's warehouse, then ransacked another near the corner of Market and Elm Streets that held

Here, along Elm Street in downtown Greensboro, unruly cavalry and starving civilians looted government storehouses. Infantry moved in to restore order, and shots were fired—some of the last of the war—against fellow Confederate soldiers. (bd)

supplies for the state. The rampaging mob included deserters and stragglers from Johnston's infantry, cavalry who did not feel compelled to continue the retreat, paroled men from Appomattox who had drifted into town, civilians bent on getting their hands on supplies, runaway slaves, and every category of refugee and displaced person that could be imagined. Leading the charge were Kentucky and Tennessee cavalrymen. Bacon, sugar, blankets, shoes, cloth, and corn were among the goods stolen.

Beauregard ordered a trusted North Carolina unit to deal with the mob, and the soldiers fired into them—the last shots fired by these troops were, ironically, at other Confederate soldiers. "[A] certain cowardly Lieut. Mollowy, of the North Carolina State troops, ordered his men to fire upon the others, which they did, killing James Brown, of Co. D, Eighth Tennessee Cavalry, and wounding one other soldiers," recalled one of the Tennessee troopers. "This was the last death in the regiment and his death was a cold-blooded murder, perpetuated by order of Lieut. Malloy, and caused great indignation with the cavalry, as Brown was an extra good soldier and a popular young man."

The chaos died down, and soon troops patrolled the streets of Greensboro, yet violence broke out at warehouses in nearby towns.

In their camps around Guilford, Randolph, and Davidson Counties, the men of the Army of Tennessee could only wait with anxiety as they learned that their commander was going to meet with General Sherman. Many were relieved, hoping to be released to go home. Others were bitter at the prospect of surrender. All were apprehensive about the future.

The Last Review of the Army of Tennessee

On the grounds of the Stevens house at Mitchener Station, the Army of Tennessee conducted its final reviews on April 4 and April 7.

"I witnessed to-day the saddest spectacle of my life . . ." said an aide to Gen. A. P. Stewart on April 4, "the review of the skeleton Army of Tennessee, that but one year ago was replete with men, and now filed by with tattered garments, worn out shoes, bare-footed and ranks so depleted that each color was supported by only thirty or forty men. . . . The march was so slow -- colors tattered and torn with bullets—that it looked like a funeral procession."

To visit the site, Mitchener Station is located in Selma, North Carolina, along Buffalo Road and Old Beulah Road.

The Stevens house still overlooks the grounds where the review unfolded. (dd)

The last review of the re-constituted Army of Tennessee took place in this field in early April 1865. (bd)

Mr. Bennett's Parlor

CHAPTER SIX

APRIL 17-18, 1865

On the pleasant spring morning of April 17, Generals Sherman and Johnston, accompanied by their staffs and escorts of troops, rode out from their respective lines to meet somewhere in the middle. Johnston had started from Gen. Wade Hampton's headquarters at the Dickson farm just outside of Hillsborough, while Sherman had taken a train from his headquarters in Raleigh to Durham Station, and was met there by his cavalry commander, Maj. Gen. Judson Kilpatrick.

Both groups rode along the Hillsborough Road, meeting not far from a farmhouse that Johnston's party had just passed. They decided to return there and ask the use of the home, which belonged to James and Nancy Bennett.

Like all families, the Bennetts had endured the tragedies of war. They had lost both sons, Lorenzo, dying in the ranks of the 27th North Carolina, and Alphonzo, believed to have died of illness at home. Their son-in-law, Robert Duke, serving with the 46th North Carolina, had also perished.

The Bennetts obliged the officers and waited in the kitchen with their daughter Eliza and her first-born son while the generals used the home.

While Sherman and Johnston sat down inside, their officers waited in the yard. The two cavalry chiefs, Gens. Wade Hampton and Judson Kilpatrick, were cordial at first, but quickly their discussion grew heated. Kilpatrick had been embarrassed a few weeks earlier by Hampton in a surprise attack at Monroe's Crossroads. The two men began shouting and, eventually, challenged each other to settle the dispute.

Reconstructed around the ruins of the original chimney, the Bennett home reflects the standard of living for working class farm families at the time of the war. (cm)

LEFT: Confederate Wade Hampton had commanded cavalry both in Virginia and the Carolinas. RIGHT: The commander of Sherman's cavalry, Judson Kilpatrick, had a similar—but less effective—record of service. The two cavalrymen got into a shouting match at the Bennett House while their commanders negotiated for peace. (loc)(loc)

"Each desired nothing more than that the settlement of the whole thing should be left to the cavalry in a fair fight," *New York Herald* reporter E. D. Westfall wrote. "The contagion spread among the respective cavalry staffs and these gentlemen parted without increased love for each other."

In the Bennett home, where the meetings occurred, all furnishings are reproductions. (bd)

Inside, Sherman revealed to Johnston a telegram that contained potentially catastrophic news: Abraham Lincoln had been assassinated. Johnston instantly realized it changed the entire scope of the negotiations.

Both generals wished to quickly restore peace, order, and a sense of normalcy as soon as possible. Johnston suggested that, "instead of a partial suspension of hostilities, we might, as other generals had done, arrange the terms of a permanent peace . . ." In other words, end the war, for good.

Sherman was hesitant—as he could not delve into political issues—but agreed, thinking that this was in the spirit of Lincoln's hope for a quick and smooth transition to peace. As both officers concurred in their conviction, a friendship began to form. After two hours, near sunset, they agreed to meet at noon the next day after Johnston informed President Davis of their decision.

That night in Hillsborough, Johnston, Gen. John C. Breckinridge (who was also the Confederate Secretary of War), Postmaster John C. Reagan, and Governor Zebulon Vance discussed terms they wished to propose. They produced several key points that would not only end the fighting here but end the war as a whole, restore peace, and keep the current state governments running. Not wishing to merely surrender the army, they prepared terms to restore the South on an equal footing.

The following day Breckinridge accompanied Johnston to the Bennett house, arriving at 2 p.m. Sherman objected to the participation of a member of the Confederate government, but Johnston explained Breckenridge's role was not as Secretary of War, but as a Confederate general. Sherman dropped his objections, but soon found another reason for concern. As the Confederates presented their plans, Sherman became frustrated with their proposed terms, which seemed to him to be presumptuous. "See here, gentlemen," Sherman finally interjected, "just who is doing the surrendering, anyhow?"

The war-hardened, Ohio-born general then quickly wrote out terms he felt were appropriate, incorporating the thoughts of Johnston and Breckinridge and the spirit of President Lincoln. The agreement allowed the men of the Army of Tennessee to march home and deposit their arms in state arsenals; the existing state governments would continue to be recognized as such; federal courts would be reestablished; and the property and political rights of the citizens were guaranteed. They were wide and sweeping terms.

Pre-war Vice President John C. Breckinridge served as a Confederate general and cabinet member. Sherman protested his involvement in the surrender negotiations on the basis that he could not treat with a member of a government that he did not recognize, but Johnston argued that Breckinridge was there as a Confederate officer—a loophole Sherman was glad to take advantage of because Breckinridge brought valuable political wisdom to the table. (loc)

While writing out the document, Sherman produced a bottle of bourbon from his saddlebag, offering Johnston and Breckinridge a drink. As the negotiations concluded, Sherman poured himself another drink, then returned his bottle to the saddlebag. His failure to offer a parting salute to Breckinridge or Johnston offended the Kentuckian. "General Sherman is a hog. Yessir, a hog," Breckinridge later wrote. "Did you see him take that drink by himself? No Kentucky gentleman would ever have taken away that bottle. . . . He knew we needed it and needed it badly."

Still, the terms Sherman produced were everything the two Confederates had hoped for and more. Johnston readily agreed to them, and both commanders signed off on them. As Johnston commanded the Department of the Carolinas, Georgia, and Florida, the terms would affect all troops in that region—a huge swath of Confederate territory.

After departing, Sherman sent a copy of his agreement to Washington for review by President Andrew Johnson, while General Johnston sent his news to President Davis.

James and Nancy Bennett had already been impacted by the war, with the loss of three sons. After war's end, their farm was eventually abandoned and fell into disrepair. (loc)

News of the surrender quickly spread in the Confederate ranks. Captain William Stoney, a South Carolina staff officer, recalled:

Early in the day it was reported our army was to be surrendered. This rumor was at first disregarded, but presently began to assume shape and force. The wildest excitement seized the troops. . . . Colonel Rion immediately ordered the brigade into line and urged them not to leave. . . . All the afternoon the cavalry were passing us saying they "were going out." The infantry soon became almost frantic, and in every direction were rushing to beg, borrow, buy and steal horses.

Disorganization was complete. Horses carried off after plundering the wagons. The divisions supply train was thoroughly stripped. The flags of the brigade were burned by the men in the certainty of surrender. About dark an order came from army headquarters to keep the men together, but with that day the army perished- a mob remained.

The division is being rapidly reduced in this way. They are going in large bodies and at all hours without any effort being made to stop them.

As word spread throughout the scattered camps, reaction remained mixed. "Rumor says that Gen. Johnson has surrendered his whole army," wrote Sgt. Daniel Dantzler of the 2nd South Carolina Artillery in Greensboro, who later added, "We hear that negotiations are being made for peace, and that the war is at an end, on the basic of reconstruction under the United States Constitution. Great excitement prevails in the army. Some talking one thing and some another. A great many

men are talking of quitting and striking out for home. Some have gone."

Other men greeted the news with pleasure, glad to be relieved of marching and fighting. Nearly all the men began preparing to return home.

Unfortunately, Sherman and Johnston had met just two days after Lincoln's assassination, and the mood in the North had changed greatly since the surrender at Appomattox eight days earlier. Vice President Johnston and the Northern Congress were in no mood to go lightly, and the terms from the Bennett farm were rejected due to the political issues that Sherman had no authority to negotiate.

The Bennett farm today looks much as it did in its humble heyday. (cm)

Confusion and Unrest

CHAPTER SEVEN

APRIL 25-MAY 10, 1865

On April 25, Lt. Gen. Ulysses S. Grant journeyed to Raleigh to consult with Sherman. It had been two weeks since he had overseen the surrender of Lee's army, but the more-southern latitude of the North Carolina capital made spring seem even more advanced.

Grant had been given strict orders to offer the same terms he had granted to Lee at Appomattox; otherwise, the Union army was to mobilize within 48 hours and advance on Greensboro.

But not only did Grant have to fix the situation, he also had to rescue his most trusted subordinate's reputation. The government and the Northern press had taken Sherman to serious task for the over-generosity of his negotiations. Sherman described such criticisms as "an outrage." He felt personally attacked and bitterly resented it.

Under Grant's thumb, Sherman contacted Johnston about meeting again.

Imagine Johnston's frame of mind: he had received Davis' approval for the terms, then an hour later got Sherman's message that they had been rejected by President Johnson.

In the meantime, with the truce called off, Johnston prepared his army to move. The reaction among the soldiers was one of shock: first told they were going home, now they learned their war was not yet over. "May I ever be spared such a sigh as I witnessed when the order to move was given," one soldier wrote. "Whole regiments remained on the ground, refusing to obey. In the last ten

Despite the overall tumult of the surrender negotiated there, Bennett Place today offers a place of quiet contemplation. (cm)

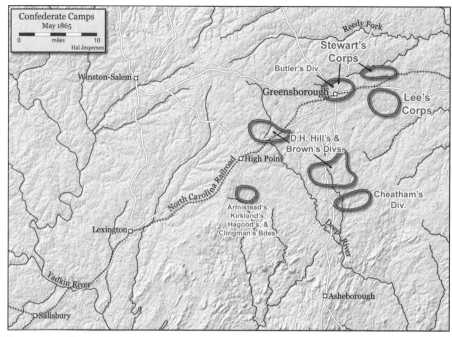

Confederate Camps—In their scattered camps, Confederate troops awaited their fate. These were tension-filled days for the veterans of many grueling campaigns. Johnston struggled to hold his army together in order to preserve his strength at the bargaining table, but desertion ran high.

days desertion had reduced Kirkland's brigade from 1,600 to 300 men."

Desertion, drunkenness, and general disorder were sliding the Army of Tennessee's camps into chaos across the region. South Carolina staff officer Bromfield Ridley wrote, "Around the campfires the surrender was discussed. Confusion and unrest prevailed."

The soldiers also resorted to ingenuity to meet their daily needs. Private Clement Saussy of Wheaton's Battery (GA) wrote of one adventure:

[B]y some mishap I lost my hat, and was bareheaded for two days. At that time, the Yankee prisoners were being removed from Salisbury in the box cars, with sentinels at each side door and on top of the cars. As comrade Jim Freeborn was also bareheaded, I suggested to him that we cut a long sapling so as to sweep the top of the train so as to knock off some hats from the sentinels. To this Freeborn agreed and we were soon ready for business. Very soon a train came in sight, and with a mighty effort we made the sweep and down came several hats. There owners were completely taken by surprise and fired

*several shots at us. The motion of the train made their
aim uncertain, and we escaped. When the train passed
around the curve, we descended and got two or three fairly
good hats.*

The two commanding generals realized they had to
continue negotiating before the situation dissolved into
complete turmoil. On April 26, Johnston and Sherman
met for a third time in the Bennett's small dining room.

The terms they finalized led to the largest troop
surrender of the war. Johnston's surrender not only
included the Army of Tennessee, but the Department
of the Carolinas, Georgia, and Florida, with many
garrisons, detachments, and scattered commands in
those four states. Altogether it included 89,270 men.

The terms allowed the men of the Army of
Tennessee to keep 7/8ths of their weapons; to use the
army's transportation (wagons and horses) to return
home; stipulated that the Union army would send
rations to their camps around Greensboro; and the navy
would assist those needing transportation to the Gulf
states. The men were to stack their rifles and park their
artillery where they were camped, and battle flags were
to be turned over.

However, there were no Union troops to oversee
this process; Confederates were to self-police their
own surrender.

As with Appomattox, the men were to be issued
paroles. Sherman sent Gen. William Hartstuff to
organize this effort. Arriving in Greensboro by rail, he
wrote, "[I]t was with a curious, half-uneasy sensation
that I thus for the first time found myself on the wrong
side of the Confederate outposts without having driven
them in by a hostile advance. It was not easy to orient
one's self at once with the new condition of things, and
it would hardly have been a surprise to find that we had
been entrapped by a ruse."

To provide a measure of security, one regiment, the
104th Ohio, was chosen to move into Greensboro. In the
only thing like a formal ceremony, they relieved a guard
of South Carolinians at the railroad yard in downtown
Greensboro. Private Joseph Gaskill wrote of their arrival:

*A patrol guard of Union soldiers is placed on duty in the
village to keep order while other detachments are sent to
surrounding fields where rebel guards are relieved from
duty over supplies surrendered to our forces . . . Relieving
this guard from duty over their own property is a new*

George Trenholm, secretary of the Treasury, stayed in this home, Blandwood, because he was ill. It is one of the few pre-war historic homes remaining in downtown Greensboro and is open to the public. (dd)

experience and some what embarrassing yet the change is made without friction and apparent regret on the part of the rebel guards we are relieving. The "Johnnies" knew what we are there for, so after receiving instructions from the sergeant of this guard we march along the line when the rebel guard takes proper position, instructs the 'yank' who relieves him and drops in rear of the line until all are relieved. They are then formed in line by their sergeant and stack arms on which they hang a varied assortment of equipment, break ranks and their warfare is ended.

Guarding those trains was Pvt. George Bussey of the 7th South Carolina Consolidated Regiment, who wrote:

It fell to my lot to be on post when the enemy came to relive us. ..In a short time a detail was sent to relieve me. I simply gave the man direction as to what I was there for, and bade him adieu. They didn't' take my gun or anything that I had. I walked leisurely alone down the railroad in the direction our regiment had gone, meditating upon what had happened and that the terrible fight was all over with, as it could not be helped and we had done all that a brave people could do, and felt relieved and glad that we were going home.

By May 3, the men of the Army of Tennessee were on their way home, flooding the roads south and west of Greensboro. The army officially paroled about 36,000 men, yet it had started the campaign in early April with close to 60,000. Included in the ranks were men from every Confederate state, as well as Missouri, Maryland,

This building, the Court House for Johnston County, North Carolina, is the third to stand on this site. While pursuing Johnston's army across the state, William Tecumseh Sherman used the second building as his headquarters. It was there on April 12, 1865, that Sherman announced to his men the surrender of Robert E. Lee's Army of Northern Virginia. (dd)

and Kentucky. The men of Johnston's army received $1.17 in pay, and many used yarn or cloth to barter for food as they journeyed home.

Feeling overwhelmed in Greensboro, the 104th Ohio was joined by the 9th New Jersey to help maintain order. Union troops and officers got along fairly well with the residents of Greensboro, and there were no altercations with former Confederate soldiers. Many Union officers enjoyed visiting the site of the Revolutionary War battle of Guilford Courthouse, about six miles from downtown Greensboro.

Not all terms of the surrender were observed. The 1st Georgia not only kept their flag, but openly flew it as they marched home. "The Regiment marched back to Ga with its colors flying, and disbanded at Augusta," wrote the unit's colonel, Charles Olmstead. "I brought the flags home with me."

*   *   *

Included in the transaction at Bennett Place was the Confederate garrison at Jacksonville, Florida. On May 10, Union Maj. Gen. Edward M. McCook arrived in Tallahassee with a division of cavalry to accept Confederate Maj. Gen. Samuel Jones' surrender of all Confederate forces in Florida. In a formal ceremony held there on May 20, McCook ordered the United States flag to be raised over the capitol, and announced the Emancipation Proclamation. Florida's state capital was the only one east of the Mississippi to not fall to Union forces during the war (the only other capital spared capture was Austin, Texas).

"At Tallahassee the flag was saluted, as it rose, with a gun for every State of the indivisible Union, and at sunset, when drawn down, with a hundred guns," the *Cincinnati Commercial* reported. "The soldiers and negroes

One of the few reminders of the Civil War in downtown Greensboro, these monuments at the corner of South Elm and Smothers Place commemorate the Army of Tennessee's stay in the area. This was also where Johnston gave his farewell address to the troops. (bd)

were in ecstacy; the citizens were not so enthusiastic, but some of them removed their hats in token."

In Florida, 8,000 troops laid down their arms. The captured supplies included 40 guns, 25,000 arms, 1,200 cartridge boxes, 63,000 pounds of lead, 100,000 round of artillery ammunition, 112,900 rounds of small arms ammunition, 70 horses, 80 mules, and 40 wagons.

Because Johnston command included the Carolinas, Georgia, Florida, and Tennessee, Union commanders across the region had to take into account the scattered commands and garrisons of Johnston's department, as well as men on detached duty, in hospitals, on furlough, etc. Union troops moved out across the southeastern states to issue paroles and the oath of allegiance to these scattered Confederate forces.

*   *   *

Cavalrymen Wade Hampton and Joseph Wheeler were in no mood to surrender.

The two generals took as many fast-moving cavalry as they could out of the camps around Greensboro and went south, as Davis intended the entire army to do. Wheeler raced to catch up with Davis and his escort—still trying to make a getaway south and west to reestablish the Confederate government—while Hampton went through the heart of South Carolina to join other forces.

However, Wheeler and his men were captured by

Union patrols while camped near Augusta, Georgia, on May 9. Hampton reached Yorkville, South Carolina, on May 1, where, dejected and exhausted, he called it off. The few who had made it that far went to their homes.

"One by one they had fallen away," Wheeler later wrote, "some begging off on account of their families, others alleging that their horses could go no farther. Their spirit was gone, they felt that the expedition was without a purpose or hope. Their heart was not in what they were dong, and seeing this realizing that all efforts were in vain, the general let them go."

One Confederate soldier who escaped the encirclement at Appomattox was James Albright. Reaching Greensboro, his hometown, he hoped to keep fighting only to learn that surrender negotiations were underway. Ironically, he owned a print shop and was asked to print the paroles. Thus a soldier from the Army of Northern Virginia oversaw printing of paroles for the Army of Tennessee.

Union troops moved into western North Carolina in May to occupy key points. In a warehouse in Charlotte, they found documents from the Confederate War Department, as well as boxes of captured Union battleflags, which were sent to Washington.

Because the armies were camped in different locations and the negotiations and distribution of paroles also occurred in different areas, accounts from participants mention the surrender taking place at Durham Station, Greensboro, Bennett Place, and elsewhere.

The men who participated in the largest troop surrender of the war did not agree on its name.

Maj. Gen. Joseph Wheeler's performance as a cavarly commander in the Western Theater has largely been overshadowed by that of his contemporary, Lt. Gen. Nathan Bedford Forrest. A competent and hard fighter, he was a poor disciplinarian, and his men were as much a scourge on the Georgia population as Sherman's armies were during the March to the Sea. (loc)

To visit sites associated with the surrender in North Carolina:

Bennett Place State Historic Site
4409 Bennett Memorial Rd.
Durham, NC 27705

Blandwood
447 W Washington St.
Greensboro, NC 27401

Greensboro Historical Museum
130 Summit Ave.
Greensboro, NC 27401

North Carolina Museum of History
5 E Edenton St.
Raleigh, NC 27601

Averasboro Battlefield Museum
3300 NC Highway 82
Dunn, NC 28334

Bentonville Battlefield State Historic Site
5466 Harper House Rd.
Four Oaks, N.C. 27524

Descending Into Chaos

CHAPTER EIGHT

APRIL-MAY 1865

Simultaneous events occurred across the south that spring at a dizzying pace. As Davis and his party left Richmond for Danville on the evening of April 2, they discussed plans to continue the war, regrouping wherever and however they needed to.

Yet the Confederacy was crumbling fast.

On April 1, Florida Governor John Milton took his own life at his plantation home in Jackson County rather than face the impending end of the war.

In Alabama, on March 22, Maj. Gen. James Wilson launched a cavalry raid that penetrated the interior of the state, one of the last large areas untouched by Union forces.

In Danville, Virginia, on April 3, the government set up a new capital with the intention of permanently reasserting itself. Davis stayed at the Sutherlin Mansion, and he and his cabinet agreed to run the war from here unless Lee was defeated. Davis himself stated he would "not leave Virginia until Lee was whipped out of it"

When asked if the Confederacy was defeated, Davis replied, "By no means. We'll fight it out to the Mississippi River." Yet the news from Lee's army was not good, and plans were made to move to Charlotte, North Carolina, to continue running the war from there. Accordingly, War Department clerks were sent ahead to make preparations in that city.

"Danville is in a perfect uproar," observed Pvt. John Dooley of the 1st Virginia, who had been convalescing there.

The streets are choked with government wagons trying

From April 3-10, 1865, Danville, Virginia, served as the third Confederate capital. The first had been Montgomery, Alabama, in the earliest days of the war, and Richmond had served as the second. After Danville, the Confederate capital would be a moving target as Davis fled ever deeper into the South's interior. (bd)

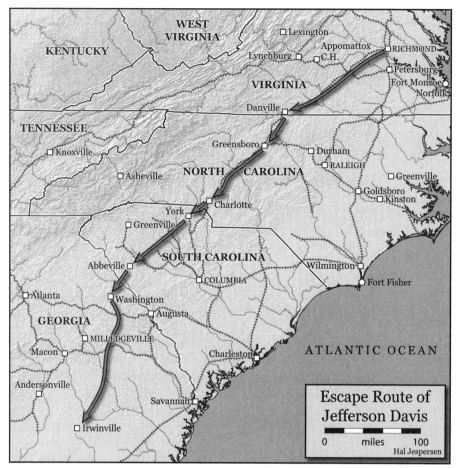

ESCAPE ROUTE OF JEFFERSON DAVIS—After fleeing Richmond on the night of April 2, Davis moved the Confederate capital to Dansville, Virginia, where he awaited word from Lee about the state of military affairs. The surrender at Appomattox made Danville untenable, so Davis retreated farther and farther into the Confederate interior. There were several close calls with Union forces, but Davis and his party managed to get to southern Georgia before being captured.

to force their way out of town. Soldiers and officers of every degree and description throng the town, mingled in one promiscuous mass, every one asking and but few answering. Some hurry to take this road, saying it is safer, others seek an exit from the opposite side of town. Here is an immense crowd at the depot, and they are carrying off everything transportable- bales of cotton, wool, bundles of raw cotton, boxes of licorice.

Davis and his cabinet stayed in Danville until the 10th, when they had confirmation of Lee's surrender. That same day, reports of Union cavalry in the area forced them to move. Travelling south, the government's

As a former Congressman, a decorated Mexican War hero, a former secretary of war, and U.S. senator, Jefferson Davis (left) looked far more qualified, on paper, to serve as a chief executive than Abraham Lincoln. His future wife, Varina (right), who was eighteen years his junior, had a mixed impression when she first met him: "He impresses me as a remarkable kind of man, but of uncertain temper, and has a way of taking for granted that everybody agrees with him when he expresses an opinion, which offends me; yet he is most agreeable and has a peculiarly sweet voice and a winning manner of asserting himself." They were engaged a month later. (loc)(loc)

next destination on the way to Charlotte was Greensboro, North Carolina, where they received a lukewarm reception. Davis stayed at the home of his aide John T. Wood, while the cabinet members stayed on the railroad cars in the rail yard.

"No provision had been made for the accommodation of the President and staff or for his cabinet," wrote Secretary of the Navy Stephen R. Mallory, "and to their surprise they found it impracticable to obtain these essentials, important alike to peasant and potentates, board and lodging." He continued:

Greensboro had been a flourishing town, and there were many commodious and well furnished residences in and about it; but their doors were closed and their "latch strings pulled in" against the members of a retreating government. The President was unwell, and Col. Wood of his staff provided him with a bed at the limited and temporary quarters of his family, and the staff and cabinet, with other prominent gentleman, took up their quarters in a dilapidated, leaky passenger car. Here they ate, slept, and lived during the day. Among the generous people of Greensboro, a negro boy cooking their rations in the open air near them. Mr. Trenholm, who was very ill, and who found quarters at the large and elegant mansion of Gov. Morehead, was the only exception.

While in Greensboro, Davis discussed several options with Johnston, including moving the Army of Tennessee to the southwest. When that was deemed impractical, Davis considered taking only the cavalry. Even as he finally gave Johnston and Beauregard reluctant approval to meet with Sherman, Davis prepared to move again. Meanwhile, Breckenridge spent a day with Johnston and Sherman before continuing on with the president and the movement south.

"From what I have seen and learned . . ." Lee wrote to Davis on April 20, "the country east of the Mississippi is morally and physically unable to maintain the contest unaided with any hope of success." In the midst of his flight southward, Davis never received the letter. Instead, his morale and the morale of his cabinet remained high. "Indeed," said one observer, "we were all in good spirits under adverse circumstances." (ncdah)(ncdah)

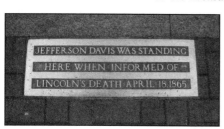

In Charlotte, news reached Davis of Lincoln's assassination. Many vengeful Northerners were already calling to have Davis hanged in connection with the assasination plot, although Davis knew nothing of it. (hmdb. org/td)

On April 13, Davis received Lee's letter explaining the surrender at Appomattox. The mood now changed. Davis alone wanted to continue the war. While the cabinet disagreed with him, they continued to move onward toward Charlotte. However, the railroad leading south was cut by Union cavalryman George Stoneman, so the party moved on in wagons. Their escort consisted of a brigade each of Tennessee and Kentucky cavalry.

Unknown to Davis, on April 14, Lt. Gen. Richard Taylor sent a message from his headquarters in Meridian, Mississippi, asking for instructions because the fall of Mobile on the 12th had altered his strategic situation. With no reply, Taylor tried again on April 20, but was again left in the dark.

In Charlotte, Davis stayed at the home of Lewis Bates on the corner of Tryon and Fourth Street. There, he got news of Johnston's treaty with Sherman, which he approved. When news of its rejection by the Washington government arrived, Davis advised Johnston to "retire with his cavalry, and as many infantry as could be mounted" and move south. Davis intended to go to the Trans-Mississippi and unite the forces of Gen. Richard Taylor in Mississippi and Alabama with those of Gen. Kirby Smith to the west of the great river. This, of course, Johnston rejected—and instead negotiated the final terms of surrender at the Bennett farm.

Also in Charlotte, Attorney General George Davis departed. With his home of Wilmington now in Federal hands, he wanted to attend to his affairs.

Crossing into South Carolina, the group stayed at the home of Col. A. B. Springs in Fort Mill. There, Secretary of the Treasury George A. Trenholm left the party.

The group moved on through York, Union, and onto Abbeville, near the Georgia state line.

Meeting at the Burt house in Abbeville, Davis broke up the government, as it was unable to function. Still, he wanted to continue the struggle. "None of them knew what was going on, what was going to be done, or what ought to be done," wrote Gen. Basil Duke of the meeting. Mallory reigned as Secretary of the Navy. Despite all the gloom, one observer said Davis "seemed in excellent sprits."

The remaining party left Abbeville at 11 p.m. on May 2 for Washington, Georgia. That same day, the Federal government offered a reward of $100,000 for the capture of Jefferson Davis.

Like a string of "George Washington slept here" signs, historical markers in four states trace Davis's flight and the many death throes of the Confederate government that took place along the way. "During much of the journey," said one participant, "Mr. Davis was singularly equable and cheerful; he seemed to have had a great load taken from his mind . . . and his conversation was bright and agreeable." His mood sombered when he received news of Lincoln's death. (mm)(mm)(bd)(mm)

Upon reaching Washington, the treasury was divided to pay the cavalry escort, and some was turned over to Richmond bank representatives for safety. A trooper in the 8th Tennessee Cavalry noted that $108,000 was divided among them: each man got $26.25. Davis took $30,000 to cover his travel expenses, and another $60,000 went hidden in a false-bottomed wagon to Charleston, where it was to be sent to England and smuggled to the Confederate government once it relocated to Texas.

Davis decided to move to the Trans-Mississippi to continue the war, and since a small group could move faster, much of the remaining cavalry was dismissed. The three remaining cabinet members— Postmaster Reagan, Secretary of War Breckinridge (who had rejoined the group), and Secretary of State Judah Benjamin—all departed, as well. The same day, President Lincoln was buried in Springfield, Illinois.

Erected in 1915 by the United Daughters of the Confederacy, a monument commemorating the last meetings of the Confederate cabinet sits on South Tryon Street at the intersection of West 3rd Street in Charlotte. Despite the marker's claim, the cabinet continued to meet after it left Charlotte. Approximately 300 feet away, at the corner of 4th Street and South Tryon Street, a bronze plaque is set in the sidewalk marking the spot where Jefferson Davis heard news of Lincoln's assasination. (hmdb.org/sth)

Davis had hoped to join his wife Varna's party, which was a few days ahead of his. They united on May 8 and kept moving, with only a 10-man cavalry escort.

Having separated from Davis and his entourage, Brig. Gen. Samuel W. Ferguson's cavalry crossed to Savannah and sent out scouts to find a Union force to surrender to. His troopers were distributing Confederate gold among themselves.

At Irwinville on May 10, the 4th Michigan Cavalry and 1st Wisconsin Cavalry closed in on the Davises and their party. Riding into their camp that morning, they captured the group, though not before friendly fire took the lives of two Union cavalrymen.

As the Union troopers took Davis to Macon, they called out to passing former Confederate soldiers going home, "Hey Johnny Reb, we've got your President." One quick-witted southerner replied, "Yes, and the devil's got yours."

*   *   *

Across Virginia and the Carolinas, separated and isolated units began to hear the news of the surrenders and seek out the nearest Union troops for surrender and parole. Or they just went home. The 60th Virginia received news of Appomattox on April 11, and disbanded the next day in their camp at Christiansburg.

On April 20 at Macon, Georgia, Maj. Gen. Howell Cobb surrendered 1,200 Georgia militia. The following day Union troops there received orders from Sherman to "desist from further acts of war and destruction until you hear that hostilities are resumed."

In Weldon, North Carolina, the 13th Battalion North Carolina Artillery, about 300 men now acting as infantry, tried to avoid, "the giant arms of an octopus." They were constantly on the move to avoid Union patrols, waiting for news from Lee or Johnston. On April 12 they left for Raleigh, and Pvt. James Mullen noted that Weldon's citizens were "panic stricken" at their withdrawal. They soon met a paroled soldier from the Army of Northern Virginia, thus learning about Appomattox. On April 12 they entered Ridgeway, and two days later arrived at Arpsboro, where they heard of Johnston's surrender. Here they sent a flag truce to Union forces in Raleigh, and by April 21 were headed home.

Also on April 21 Col. John S. Mosby arranged a truce and secured his parole. His force, one of the Confederacy's most successful, disbanded at Millwood in northern Virginia. In Chester, South Carolina, the 2nd South Carolina Cavalry, isolated and cut off, also disbanded.

One of the Confederacy's most famous units, the Kentucky troops of the Orphan Brigade, also endured a long odyssey during these weeks. Hearing rumors of an armistice, one soldier wrote, "our worst fears were confirmed." The Orphans moved from Camden, South

"This corner has probably witnesed the passing of more historic men than any spot in the up country of South Carolina," says a monument at the intersectin of W. Liberty St. and S. Congress St. in York, South Carolina. Through the crossroads passed militia during the Revolution. During the last days of the Civil War, Davis and his party spent the night at the nearby Rose Hotel, where Secretary of State Judah Benjamin gave a speech to the assembled citizens. General Wade Hampton passed by, as well, trying to take his remaining cavalry to the Trans-Mississippi. (hmdb.org/sth)

Jefferson Davis Memorial Historic Site in Irwinville, Georgia, preserves the campsite where the presidential party was captured. The 13-acre park features a monument on the exact spot of Davis' capture, erected in 1936 by the United Daughters of the Confederacy. The park also includes a Civil War museum. (loc)

In the confusion of the early morning attack, Davis had thrown his wife's overcoat over his shoulders. The Northern press had a field day with the incident, printing many cartoons and articles depicting Davis in women's clothing. It even inspired a catchy song. (loc)

Carolina, to Augusta, Georgia, arriving on May 2. During these days, they saw Lee's men pass through the region. Davis also passed by, determined to continue the war.

But in Augusta, they learned that "the last hope of success has vanished." Their commander thanked them for "your suffering and your fortitude in the camp and your gallantry on the field of battle."

On May 4, 17,000 rations arrived in Augusta, along with troops from the Union XIX Corps. They took control of the 60,000 pounds of gunpowder in the magazine there.

The Kentuckians prepared for surrender. "The Orphans marched down the streets in closed column, flags flying in their tatters, arms at the parade position," wrote Pvt. John S. Jackman. "The towns people came to the boardwalks to watch them as if on review." As they marched in, the 13th Tennessee Cavalry (US) entered from the other side, and Jackman wrote, "It looked strange not to see them commence shooting at each other." Their weapons were taken to Union headquarters, "piling them in a heap," and on May 7, they got their paroles. Thus in Augusta, Confederate troops from a border state surrendered to Union troops from a southern state. Union general Emory Upton soon arrived in town to oversee the continuing parole process.

On May 9, the same day Upton arrived in Augusta, newly appointed President Andrew Johnson issued a proclamation declaring that armed resistance was "virtually" at an end. Still, all over the South, the unraveling continued.

In North Carolina, Capt. Halcott P. Jones of the 13th Battalion North Carolina Artillery moved from his native state with some of the battery southward into South Carolina. In late April, they disbanded at Chester. "It was a sad sight to see the old guns that I had been with so long laying battered about in the midst of a complete wreck of carriages ammunition and equipments," he said. "I parted . . . and started to go with Gen. Bragg to the Trans-Miss. Or to Ala." Jones got as far as Abbeville where, like many, "finding it impracticable to get to Alabama, I concluded to return home."

Brigadier General B. J. Hill took his two regiments of locally raised north Georgia and northern Alabama troops from Jacksonville, Alabama, to Dalton, Georgia, seeking out the nearest Union troops. Now that the Army of Tennessee had surrendered, they asked to do the same, and were told to move to Villanow, Georgia, on May 20 where they were paroled.

At Quallatown, North Carolina, Col. W. H. Thomas, commanding the 69th and 80th North Carolina, gathered about 300 men from other commands and moved to Waynesville. They skirmished with Federal troops on May 9, then, upon learning of the larger situation, surrendered.

On May 11, members of the 4th Iowa Cavalry arrested Confederate Vice President Alexander Stephens in Georgia. The next day at Kingston, Georgia, 3,000 men under Gen. William T. Wofford surrendered to Gen. Henry M Judah. Wofford had about 10,000 soldiers under his command, "on paper," consisting of all the Confederate troops in northwestern Georgia; however, only about a third were on hand—the rest had deserted. As was standard practice, the Confederate soldiers received rations after surrendering.

Perhaps the last troops east of the Mississippi to surrender were those of a detachment of the 80th North Carolina under Maj. Stephen Whitaker. They laid down their arms near Franklin, North Carolina, on May 14.

Florida was another chaotic area, wrote one Tallahassee resident: "The air was full of rumors of defeat, victories, terms of peace, unconditional surrender, European interference, etc. Everywhere the unsettled state of the country provoked deeds of lawlessness."

On May 20, the United States flag rose over Tallahassee accompanied by a cannon salute for every state in the Union. "The soldiers and Negros were in ecstasy," wrote one observer, "the citizens were not so enthusiastic, but some of them removed their hats in token."

The Fall of Mobile

CHAPTER NINE

APRIL 12, 1865

Since the early days of the war, Federals had targeted Mobile with little success. Finally, in August 1864, with Rear Admiral David G. Farragut "damning the torpedoes," the Federal Navy captured Mobile Bay. While they still did not capture the city, Federals effectively closed it off, finally sealing the blockade along the Gulf Coast. The anchor from Farragut's flagship, the U.S.S. *Hartford,* now sits on display in Fort Gaines, one of the forts that guarded the bay. (gm)

Warm spring breezes from the Gulf swept through the streets of Mobile, Alabama. This old colonial port, controlled previously by the French, Spanish, and British, would now become the center of attention following the surrenders in Virginia and North Carolina.

After the battle of Mobile Bay in August 1864, Union forces under Maj. Gen. Edward R. S. Canby concentrated around the city, preparing to attack its fortifications. Despite the Union naval victory in the bay, its landward defenses had to be reduced in order to take the city. Canby commanded the Department of West Mississippi, which included Union forces in Arkansas, Mississippi, Alabama, Texas, and Louisiana. This one general would oversee the final major surrenders of the war.

Born in Kentucky, Edward Richard Sprigg Canby served in the Seminole and Mexican Wars before the Civil War broke out in 1861. His victory in New Mexico in 1862 secured the southwest for Union forces, and he later served in various areas, including New York City. In 1864, he was assigned to Louisiana, as a proven Union general with a competent record of achievement.

Also born in Kentucky, Lt. Gen. Richard Taylor was the son of President Zachary Taylor. He had fought in the east with the Army of Northern Virginia in 1862, and was then transferred to Louisiana, where he rose to departmental command by 1865.

Mobile was defended on the west by a ring of fortifications and on the east by Spanish Fort and Fort Blakely—both across the bay from the city. Taylor, commanding the Department of Alabama, Mississippi,

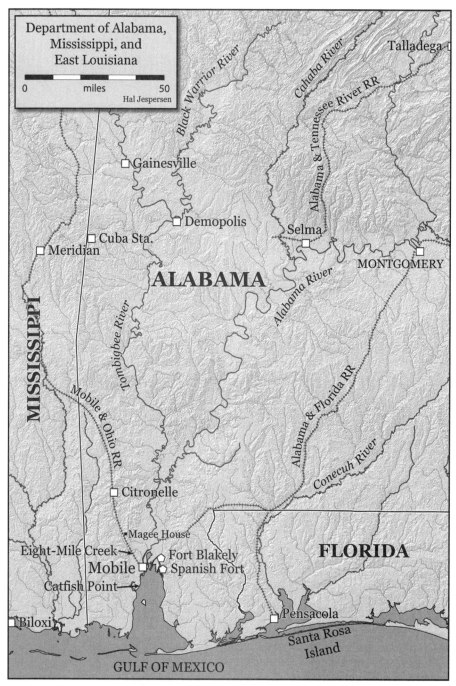

DEPARTMENT OF ALABAMA, MISSISSIPPI, AND EAST LOUISIANA—Gen. Richard General Taylor's forces were concentrated around Meridian, Mississippi, and Demopolis, Alabama. However, a garrison of troops under his overall authority, commanded by Brig. Gen. Dabney Maury, still held the important city of Mobile. The fall of the city dramatically altered the strategic situation in the department for Taylor, who began to look for an honorable way to spare his troops.

LEFT: One of the Union army's most capable generals, Edward Canby oversaw the last two major surrenders of the war. (loc) RIGHT: Commanding the Department of Mississippi, Alabama, and East Louisiana, Richard Taylor attempted to surrender with the dignity befitting the son of one of America's most notable war heroes. (loc)

and East Louisiana, made his headquarters at Meridian, Mississippi, 90 miles to the northwest. Meridian is often overlooked for its role in the Civil War. Joseph Johnston made his headquarters there in 1863 during the Vicksburg campaign, and the town was a vital crossroads, railroad junction, and supply depot.

Brigadier General Dabney Maury commanded the Mobile garrison. A Mexican War veteran, he had seen action in Arkansas, Mississippi, and Tennessee prior to commanding in Mobile.

Maury had been trying to get as many troops as he could to defend the city as Union forces built up in the region in an obvious attempt to take it. Alabama Governor Thomas Watts insisted that, should the city be evacuated, it must be left "a heap of ashes." The Mobile garrison had been increased to about 9,000 men by the spring of 1865,

Fort Morgan once helped guard Mobile Bay, but it fell into Federal hands in August of 1864. In April of 1865, Federals used it as their staging ground for an attack against Mobile itself, starting with an assault on Fort Blakely. (gm)

and it was augmented by Alabama militia, which rotated shifts in the city's defenses. Ammunition, food, and other supplies were stockpiled in the city, and its defenses were constantly improved in preparation for a siege.

Disease and desertion were increasing problems for Maury. When Maury requested reinforcements, he noted that he preferred troops "not connected by any ties" to Mobile or Alabama in order to decrease the chances that they'd slip away for home.

Mobile was an important port and manufacturing center for the Confederacy. The city had several hospitals; printing facilities that produced, among other things, money and postage stamps; and a railroad center. There

Left: Brig. Gen. Dabney Maury, commander of the Mobile garrison, was one of Taylor's key subordinates. (loc) Right: Commodore Ebenezer Farand commanded Confederate naval forces around Mobile Alabama. (na)

were also significant naval stores and shipbuilding facilities in the area. The C.S.S. *Hunley* had been built here, and many naval experiments had been conducted offshore.

Unlike the surrenders in Virginia and North Carolina, naval forces played a significant role in Alabama. Commodore Ebenezer Farrand's Confederate naval forces included the ironclad rams *Nashville* and *Tuscumbia*, as well as the side-wheel steamer *Morgan*.

Aside from Mobile, Canby's other targets were Selma and Montgomery. The capture and destruction of industrial centers, railroads, and crops in central Alabama would cripple the Confederacy's remaining war capability.

*   *   *

Canby's command included the XIII and XVI Corps, and their offensive began in late March. He led 32,000 Union troops against Fort Blakely and Spanish Fort on the eastern side of Mobile Bay. Union troops first overran a Confederate outpost at Fort Blakeley on April 1; the next day, the Federals moved in to surround the fort.

On the night of April 8, Confederate defenders evacuated, leaving only a picket line and artillery left to be captured. They walked silently without shoes along a narrow treadway just over a foot wide. They filed silently for 1,200 yards to awaiting ships.

Union troops landed here after crossing Mobile Bay, and marched in to take the city unopposed. (bd)

On the afternoon of April 9, while Lee was meeting with Grant, and Johnston was reorganizing the Army of Tennessee, Union troops attacked Fort Blakeley. They pierced the defenses, capturing about 3,400 prisoners; only about 200 Confederates escaped through the waterways.

Maury not only lost half his defending force, but also had to evacuate Mobile. The loss of the forts made the city indefensible. The news made its 40,000 residents panic. On April 10, the militia was called out and supplies were prepared for movement to Meridian. "Every body is excited and running," noted one of the Catholic nuns working in the city hospital, Sister Gabriella.

Troops dumped excess gunpowder in the bay and removed the elevation screws from the guns they could not remove (rather than spike them). Many horses and mules were impressed by Maury's soldiers to move their artillery and wagons. "Mobile was left with great reluctance by both officers and men," Taylor wrote. "The men, however, though low-spirited, behaved well."

On the morning of April 12—while the Army of Northern Virginia was laying down its rifles and the Army of Tennessee was moving west through Raleigh—Maj. Gen. Dabney Maury left the city of Mobile with the rear guard. The 12th Mississippi Cavalry was the last unit to depart. On their way out, troops set fire to bales of cotton stacked north of the city, but soon residents and home guard troops saved it, knowing its value to the enemy. Meanwhile, a volunteer guard of citizens formed to protect the remaining Confederate commissary supplies from looting.

At 10:30 that morning, two Union divisions under Maj. Gen. Gordon Granger crossed the bay and landed at Catfish Point, about five miles below the city. An impressive flotilla of six ships transported the soldiers across the wide, calm waters.

The first unit to enter the city was the 8th Illinois Infantry. They marched in and occupied Mobile around noon. Mayor R. H. Slough met the Union troops at the Magnolia Racetrack to surrender the city, using a large white sheet as a flag of truce. That afternoon, Union troops spread out in Mobile, occupying the abandoned trenches. They took possession of 150 artillery guns, thousands of small arms, 20,000 bales of cotton, 25,000

Gordon Granger's Union troops fanned out across central Alabama following the capture of Mobile. (loc)

As Maury's men marched north along the road to Citronelle and onto Meridian, they passed by the prominent home of banker Jacob Magee at the Kushla railroad stop. The site would take on extra importance in the days to come. (bg)

barrels of resin, and several vessels. Their bands filled the air with patriotic music.

Colonel Conrad Kreuz of the 27th Wisconsin proudly wrote that his unit had done "its fair share in closing the last campaign of any magnitude in the present rebellion."

The Mobile Daily News reported that the occupation went smoothly, and that United States flags soon flew over the city's public buildings. "Long may it wave," commented the editor.

*   *   *

As Canby first made his preparations to assault Mobile, Union Maj. Gen. James H. Wilson began a cavalry raid on March 22 from the northwestern corner of the state. His troopers moved across central Alabama, destroying supplies and scattering any resistance in their path. The result was that Union forces had now penetrated most of Alabama and Mississippi. Taylor's ability to control territory was diminishing rapidly.

Maj. Gen. James Wilson was a hand-picked favorite of Grant who did well early in the war but who struggled in the Eastern Theater in the spring of 1864. Subsequently relocated to a less-visible front, Wilson began to once more thrive. (loc)

Yet Taylor was still doing his best to manage the war effort in his shrinking and now-isolated department. On April 4, he wired Davis for clarification on recruiting black soldiers, which had begun in Montgomery. Taylor was still getting slave labor for military work from owners in Marengo and other counties along the Alabama/Mississippi border.

That line of communication would not last long. As Canby's XIII Corps occupied Mobile, his XVI Corps left on April 14 marching north for Montgomery to complete Union control of the region. In the meantime, a force of 4,000 Union cavalry left Eufaula striking north to break up any possible communication between Taylor and Johnston, effectively severing Taylor from the government and armies to the east.

Lastly, a division of Union infantry moved up the Tombigbee River into the state's interior. Some of those men ran into Confederate cavalry trying to burn a bridge along a place called Eight Mile Creek along the Mobile and Ohio Railroad. Colonel Henry M. Day of the 91st Illinois ordered "twenty men of the skirmish line, to charge over the bridge . . . driving the enemy from his position. The pursuit was kept up for about a mile and a half, but the enemy being mounted and scattered in confusion, a farther advance was deemed useless." This was the only pursuit and engagement towards Meridian following the capture of Mobile.

Taylor's options were limited as he faced Union troops from below (Canby at Mobile) and the east (Wilson's cavalry), as well as the north (Union-held Vicksburg and Memphis). Taylor was cut off from supply, reinforcement, and communication with the bulk of the Confederacy to the east. In fact, messages to Davis for advice had gone unanswered since early April.

Confederate forces were positioned in an arc northwest of Mobile that ran from Meridian, through Cuba Station, and on to Gainesville and Demopolis. State boundaries were irrelevant; railroads, rivers, and enemy positions dictated the deployment of Taylor's forces. His forces were positioned not only to respond to any Union threat from Mobile or central Alabama, but also so as not to tax local resources too severely.

Eight Mile Creek, the site of a skirmish following the capture of Mobile, is an easier road to travel today than it was for Confederates in April 1865. (bd)

On April 12 near Mount Pleasant, northeast of Mobile, the 91st Illinois clashed with the 12th Mississippi Cavalry. The next day Union troops again engaged the 12th Mississippi Cavalry near Eight Mile Creek, above Mobile.

Union troops established a forward base at the town of Whistler, near Eight Mile Creek, west of Mobile. This would be a jump-off point for an advance on the Confederates at Meridian. With occupation came emancipation, and slaves were free to leave their owners, though many had no place to go and chose to remain.

Because the fall of Mobile had altered the strategic situation in Alabama, Taylor sent a message to Davis on April 14 from his headquarters in Meridian asking for instructions. Again he received no reply. Taylor followed up on April 20, again receiving only silence. By then, Davis was in Greensboro and out of touch with commanders in the field.

Taylor was trying to maintain control as his department unraveled. He sent a proclamation to the Alabama Militia on April 20 reading, "your section of country will no doubt be infested by roving bands of deserters and stragglers, whose efforts will be to intimidate, oppress, and plunder the citizens." He urged

Once a bastion of Confederate resistance, Mobile was the first in a series of dominos to fall in the Deep South and the Trans-Mississippi. (gm)

"a thorough organization and a proper disposition of the county militia."

Governor Isham Harris of Tennessee arrived unexpectedly with money from the Bank of Tennessee. A bank official was in charge of the funds, but Harris felt that it should be returned to Nashville. This was eventually done, and it arrived intact.

On April 25, as the Union XVI Corps reached Montgomery, an Iowa soldier noted, "the citizens did not seem very glad to see us." Another observed that the rebellion began here, as this was the first capital of the Confederacy in 1861.

Taylor wrote to Maury at Cuba Station: "Unless the troops remain intact and are relived from service by some general agreement . . . they will be hunted down like beasts of pretty, their families will be persecuted, and ruin thus entailed not only upon the soldiers themselves, but also upon thousands of defenseless Southern women and children." He urged Maury to "assure them that their safety rests solely upon all of us remaining together in an organized state, faithfully respecting public and private property, and so performing all of our duties."

Taylor noted that while other armies held out, they "owed it to our own manhood, to the memory of the dead, and to the honor of our arms, to remain steadfast to the last." The troops at Meridian reacted "not with noisy cheers, but with solemn murmurs of approval."

Yet the writing was on the wall, and the men grew despondent. Taylor himself admitted that Lee's surrender left him few options.

Upon learning of Johnston's surrender, Taylor reached out to Canby to discuss surrender. Taylor's note was sent to Mobile on April 19.

"It was but right to tell these gallant, faithful men the whole truth concerning our situation," Taylor later wrote in his memoirs, adding:

The surrender of Lee left us little hope of success; but while Johnston remained in arms we must be prepared to fight our way to him. Again, the President and civil authorities of our Government were on their way to the south, and might need our protection. Granting the cause for which we had fought to be lost, we owed it to our own manhood, to the memory of the dead, and to the honor of our arms, to remain steadfast to the last. This was received, not with noisy cheers, but solemn murmurs of approval.

Taylor also noted that the other eastern armies had surrendered, and he could not get his forces across the Mississippi to join those in the far west. Thus he resolved to seek honorable terms, "whilst still in my power to do so." He viewed the surrender with his troops in mind, hoping to "preserve their honor and best protect them and the people."

Taylor wrote:

The succeeding hours were filled with a grave responsibility, which could not be evaded or shared. Circumstances had appointed me to watch the dying agonies of a cause that had fixed the attention of the world. To my camp, as the last refuge in the storm, came many members of the Confederate Congress. These gentlemen were urged to go at once to their respective homes, and, by precept and example, teach the people to submit to the inevitable, obey the laws, and resume the peaceful occupations on which society depends. This advice was followed, and with excellent effect on public tranquility.

As the end of April approached, his goal was to "make every effort to secure an honorable and speedy cessation of hostilities."

Mr. Magee's Parlor

CHAPTER TEN

APRIL 29-MAY 4, 1865

Peace seemed to be on the horizon in the Deep South. Taylor and Canby agreed to confer between their forces at Mobile and Meridian. The impending meeting put a stop to Canby's other operations: troops destined to move to the Trans-Mississippi Theater were detained until further notice, and other units across Alabama were instructed to hold in place.

Union scouts informed Canby that there was a prominent home about 12 miles above Mobile along the railroad line. The house of Jacob and Mary Magee, one of the few in the area, was also the biggest. Built in 1848, the home had a large front porch, with entrances to the two bedrooms on either side of the front door. The two-story creole cottage-style house had five fireplaces. Nearby was the Kushla railroad stop along the Mobile and Ohio railroad line.

Fifty-four-year-old Jacob Magee had been a jailor and sheriff, then later a banker in Mobile. He also served in the Alabama state assembly. He assisted with surveying the railroad line and, during that assignment, purchased the property for his home. The complex included a post office, gristmill, general store, and bathhouse. Immediately surrounding the home were slave quarters and a kitchen.

On April 29, Canby and an escort of 2,000 cavalrymen marched north from Mobile, and waited at the Magee house. Taylor came south on the rail line. "With one officer, Colonel William Levy, I made my appearance on a hand-car, the motive power of which

The view up the lane from the porch of the Magee House (bd)

This is the site of the railroad line north of Mobile, looking south towards the city. Up this line came General Canby and his staff, twice, to meet with Taylor. (bd)

was two negros," Taylor later wrote. Union troops were drawn up waiting at the Kushla stop to meet them.

Observers noted the contrast: a large body of well-uniformed Union troops greeted the two lone Confederates on their handcar. Taylor himself noted that the situation reflected "the fortunes of our respective causes."

It is unknown if the party talked or if there was an awkward silence as the group made its way south toward Kushla. Nor do we know the thoughts racing through the minds of Taylor, Levy, and the two unnamed slaves. No doubt their visions of the future varied widely.

Arriving at the Magee house, Taylor walked through the Union troops, accompanied by Canby, up to the front of the

This is the site of Kushla Station, where General Taylor arrived by handcar while Union troops waited at attention. (bd)

home. Upon entering, they sat in the parlor, on opposite ends of a child's fold-out desk. According to family tradition, Mary Magee had moved much of their good furniture from the parlor due to fear of looting.

The meeting went quickly, as Canby offered Taylor the same terms as Appomattox and Bennett Place, and Taylor had no room to bargain. Within 10 minutes, they emerged from the parlor with a ceasefire agreement. Champagne was on hand, courtesy of Canby, and with the popping corks, Taylor noted they were "the first agreeable explosive sounds I had heard for years." The generals walked across the hall from the parlor to the dining room.

Outside, the military band struck up "Hail, Columbia," but Canby quickly ordered them to switch to "Dixie." Taylor intervened, insisting on the first tune, noting it was appropriate as they looked towards reuniting the country.

A native German officer on Canby's staff made remarks about the "ignorance and errors" of the South, and some officers tried to suppress him. Taylor, whose grandfather led the 9th Virginia in the Revolution, reminded him of the captured Hessians at Trenton, ending the conversation.

Both commanders departed and prepared to put the surrender into motion.

While the meeting was underway at the Magee house, 250 Union cavalry swept into Citronelle, between Taylor and Levy and their troops farther back, and captured a

The Magee house's original furniture, including the table, chairs, and other pieces, have remained in the parlor since 1865. (bd)

Mary Magee (top) passed away in 1882, and Jacob (above) the following year. (bg)(bg)

train and several Confederate troops. Learning that the action had occurred during a cease-fire, the Union troops released their prisoners and apologized. "The officer in charge of the party was at the time not appraised of your presence below, and that the engine and car were part of your flag," wrote Maj. James Curell to the Confederate commander. "He has received orders to leave a safe conduct at Citronelle and have every thing prepared again for your use, and to respect your escort whenever he may meet you."

It is not known if the Magees or their two daughters were all home, or if they stayed in the house while the meeting took place. None of the family apparently wrote of the incident. Canby issued orders prohibiting looting, thus allowing the furniture to be preserved. Unlike at the McLean house or Bennett farm, no items used in the surrender were carried off by Union officers. The tables and chairs were removed from the McLean house—paid for but taken nonetheless—and Bennett also lost the table and other items from his meager dining room.

The surrender did not bring fame or notoriety to Jacob Magee as it did for Wilmer McLean. No mention of the meeting on his property was made in Magee's obituary.

After the Magees died, their youngest daughter, Winifred, sold the home to Alfred Sturtevant in 1898. An Illinois professor, he distilled turpentine and later established a dairy on the farm. The home, and its furniture, were in continuous family ownership from 1848-2004.

Several bundles of Confederate money were found on the property in the 1930s, possibly left behind when the troops retreated from Mobile.

The Magee Family Cemetery. Jacob's grave is on the left, Mary's on the right. (bd)

In 2004 the Magee farm was purchased by Mobile veterinarian Ben George and a local Sons of Confederate Veterans camp. They operated the house as a museum, but low visitation forced its closure in 2010. As of this writing, the home is for sale, its fate uncertain.

As of this writing, the Magee home is no longer open to the public, but it may be seen from the outside. It is the only original building associated with a Civil War surrender. (bd)

*   *   *

The meeting at the Magee house set the tone for cooperation between Canby and Taylor. Unfortunately, the good feelings did not last long.

Just two days later, on May 1, the generals learned that the United States government had disapproved the terms offered to Johnston by Sherman. Thus the terms Canby and Taylor agreed upon were also invalid. Canby apologetically notified Taylor that their ceasefire ended in 48 hours.

"General Canby dispatched that his government disavowed the Johnston-Sherman convention, and it would be his duty to resume hostilities," Taylor wrote. "Almost at the same instant came the news of Johnston's surrender. There was no room for hesitancy. Folly and madness combined would not have justified an attempt to prolong a hopeless contest."

It was now Taylor's turn to make a crucial decision, as Johnston had done when he disobeyed Davis. Knowing that Davis had been taken prisoner in Georgia, and that Johnston and Sherman were renegotiating, Taylor reached out again to Canby.

"General Canby was informed that I desired to meet him of the purpose of negotiating a surrender of my forces," Taylor recalled, "and that Commodore Farrand, commanding the armed vessels in the Alabama River, desired to meet Rear Admiral [Henry K.] Thatcher for a similar purpose. [Citronelle], some forty miles north of Mobile, was the appointed place."

As at Greensboro, no doubt the confusion and swirling rumors were agonizing for the soldiers camped around Meridian, Gainesville, and Demopolis. The entire area was in chaos. Taylor noted, "bank stocks, bonds, all personal property, all accumulated wealth, had disappeared. Thousands of houses, farm-buildings, work-animals, flocks and herds, had been wantonly burned, killed, or carried off. The land was filled with widows and orphans crying for aid, which the universal destitution prevented them from receiving."

Confederate cavalryman Alex Moore, who had been patrolling the road near Eight Mile Creek, delivered the message about the meeting to General Canby's adjutant general. Taylor set the meeting for Col. George P. Borden's home in Citronelle, along the railroad line.

The two generals met there on May 4. Attending were Taylor and Canby and some of their staff members. Taylor's entourage included Commodore Ebenezer Farrand, Lieutenant Commander Myers, and several other officers. Union officers included Maj. Gen. Peter Osterhaus, Brig. Gen. Christopher Andrews, Admiral Henry Thatcher, Colonel Christensen, and Captains Barreet and Perkins.

The Federal party traveled from Mobile at about

The Surrender Oak (top) no longer stands, but a sign marks the spot along Celeste Road in Citronelle (bottom). For the Civil War centennial, a memorial marker was placed at the spot by the Historical Mobile Preservation Society on May 4, 1965. Each year on the first Saturday in May, Citronelle hosts the Surrender Oak Festival at the Citronelle Depot Museum. (chps)(bd)

8:30 in the morning, and in an ironic twist of fate, the two sides arrived in Citronelle in the exact opposite manner of their arrivals at the Magee farm. The federal commanders went by rail as far as Whistler, where the line was broken; from there they traveled on a handcar. Two miles below Citronelle, a Confederate train coming south met them and took them back to the town.

The assembled parties all gathered under a large oak in front of the Borden house, known as Oakenak.

If we are plagued by too many conflicting accounts for the Appomattox meeting, the problem here is a lack of any detailed accounts. A later report noted that the meeting lasted until 7:30 pm, although we don't know exactly what time they began. Nor do we know how the conference

Under a large tree at this site, Generals Taylor and Canby met to arrange for the surrender of the Department of Alabama, Mississippi, and East Louisiana. (bd)

unfolded, whether they started where they had left off at the Magee house or began all over. Did they simply follow the Appomattox and Greensboro model, or did they start anew and finally produce something similar? We may never know. The meeting was apparently pleasant, at any rate, as Farrand and Myers renewed a prewar friendship.

The officers quite possibly discussed their earlier negotiations at the Magee house, and how the ending of the ceasefire made their present work more urgent. Naval matters must have also been delved into, as recent military operations involved sizable naval forces, and the Confederates had numerous gunboats and naval personnel on area rivers.

The *Mobile News* reported on May 16:

During the rambling conversation, which became general after the terms had been arranged and signed, some laughable stories were related of the difficulties experienced by the rebel officers in procuring supplies or services on account of the distrust entertained by the population of the value of Confederate money. Capt. ____ said that he could not get his only shirt washed for $1,000 of it, and had to divide his rations with a

The surrender oak was transformed into hundreds of souvenir objects, including a sign for the Boy Scout Camp that later occupied the site. This slice from the Surrender Oak now hangs in the Citronelle Depot Museum. (bd)

sable laundress to induce her to give her attention to the shirt at all.

General Taylor admitted he had to allow his officers to receive double rations in the last few weeks—one for them to use and the surplus to allow them to barter for goods and services.

The terms produced were nearly identical to those of Appomattox and Greensboro. Men with horses could keep them, officers would retain their side arms, the Confederate soldiers would be paroled, and Taylor would retain control of railways and river steamers to help them get home. Here, unlike earlier, the terms specifically mention the men being allowed to keep their own horses, something agreed on but not written down previously. The soldiers were not be disturbed by the authority of the United States "so long as they continue to observe the condition of their paroles." Union naval forces and Union-controlled

The scant remains of the Borden house hide in the woods near the site where the Surrender Oak once stood. (bd)

railroads would also transport men to the nearest practicable point close to their homes.

After writing up the terms, Taylor signed using a pen made from a steel point, attached to a twig, dipped in ink—he did not even have a real pen. Thus the last significant Confederate force east of the Mississippi was surrendered. General Taylor wrote afterward that the terms offered by Canby were "consistent with the honor of our arms."

Ironically, as the generals and admirals were sitting down to discuss peace, John Peacock, a soldier from the

1st Florida (US) Cavalry, was killed at Wetumpka, near Montgomery, possibly the last soldier killed in action east of the Mississippi.

One thousand miles to the north, Lincoln was buried the same day in Springfield, Illinois.

The meeting at Citronelle would be the only surrender held outdoors. The large tree under which the generals met became known as the Surrender Oak, and was a local landmark until it fell in the hurricane of 1906. After the Surrender Oak fell, the wood was cut up for gavels, walking canes, and other souvenirs. Several pieces are in the Smithsonian in Washington. The site of the tree was marked with a state historic marker, but later the marker was moved to be closer to the road.

The Citronelle Depot Museum is operated by the Citronelle Historical Preservation Society. (chps)

The Borden house burned after the war, and the home's foundations are now overgrown but still visible in the woods. The property was owned by Col. W. D. Mann of New York City, and he donated it to the Citronelle Business Men's Association. A Boy Scout camp, Camp Pushmataha, was established at the site in the 1930s. Today the property is owned by the city of Citronelle, with an interpretive marker near the state historic marker.

To visit sites associated with the surrenders in Alabama:

Citronelle Depot Museum
P.O. Box 384
Citronelle, AL 36522

Several Civil War cannons, rescued from destruction, rest at the Magee Farm. (bd)

Museum of Mobile
111 S Royal St
Mobile, AL 36602

C.S.A

ON THIS SPOT
GENERAL NATHAN
BEDFORD FORREST
AND HIS DARING
FOLLOWERS
WERE PAROLED BY
GENERAL CANBY U.S.A.
MAY 15 1865
GENERAL ARMSTEAD
AND HIS BRAVE MEN WERE

Under the Spreading Oak

CHAPTER ELEVEN
MAY 1865

Along the Tombigbee River, east of Meridian, sat a potential disaster: thousands of bales of cotton—Confederate government property—with only a treasury agent in charge. Cotton was both a blessing and a curse. It was the Confederacy's cash crop for supplies during the war. As the conflict unfolded, politicians and generals of both sides seized the commodity for personal profit. Its value increased manifold during the war. A large stash of undefended cotton was an invitation for trouble.

Taylor wanted the cotton protected and transferred quickly. Canby agreed. The Union commander arranged for a federal treasury agent from New Orleans to remove it.

Back in Meridian, Governors Charles Clarke of Mississippi and Thomas Watts of Alabama asked Taylor for advice on the military situation. He advised that they convene their legislatures, repeal secession, abolish slavery, and prepare for the transition to Union military occupation. Both were arrested by Union troops before taking any action. It is unlikely they could have acted, as the situation was too chaotic and state leaders too scattered.

With the surrender terms agreed on, the scattered troops were put in motion, concentrating at Meridian to turn in their military equipment and receive their paroles. As Johnston did in North Carolina, Taylor remained at his headquarters in Meridian until his men had all received their paroles and were on the way home.

On May 6 Taylor ordered Maury to move his

Commemorating the surrender of Nathan Bedford Forest, this monument sits on a bluff above the Tombigbee River in Gainesville, Alabama. (bd)

command to Meridian, and the troops in Cuba Station, Demopolis, and Moscow began to break camp. "You will explain to your troops," Taylor wrote to Maury, "that a surrender . . . will not be the consequence of any defeat . . . but is simply, so far as we are concerned, yielding upon the best terms and with a preservation of as much military honor to the logic of events. The cause for which we have struggled for four years was a just one at the beginning of the war and it is as just now. Say to them that their fate will be mine."

Public property at Demopolis and Cuba Station was left under the care of detached guards until Union troops arrived to take over. At 5:00 a.m. the next day, Maury's troops began marching to Meridian. "Everything was perfectly businesslike and humdrum [,] no excitement, no disorder," wrote H. H. T. Stephenson of the Washington Artillery. "The Federal troops were kept well in hand, were not allowed to insult us, and they showed no disposition to do so." Canby himself issued stern orders against looting.

Other troops departed Coffeyville, Braggs Bluff, and Elm Bluff for their final camps. Taylor made contact with railroad officials to secure use of the rails to transport the troops.

The members of the Washington Artillery of New Orleans rode the Mobile and Ohio railroad back to Mobile, and there they were presented to Canby. Lieutenant Johnson overheard the Union commander state to a fellow officer, "There is the noblest body of men that ever lived." Canby arranged for their transportation by steamer to their native city.

Perhaps the farthest from home were the Confederate artillerymen of the 3rd Maryland, who were part of the army at Meridian. After receiving their paroles, they began their long journey home.

*   *   *

On May 9, troops of the XVI Corps in Montgomery received a message from Washington that Jefferson Davis was trying to get to the Trans-Mississippi with the Confederate Treasury. "Every effort will be made to capture him with his plunder," the message said. Increased patrols watched for Davis "should he attempt to escape by passing anywhere in that region."

The next day Canby sent troops to Demopolis, Gainesville, and Meridian to oversee the surrender of the Confederates there. These troops were also ordered to protect civilians and public property "against depredations from evil-disposed persons." Foraging was "strictly prohibited" in these areas and civilians were "at all times treated with discretion and respect."

Confederate civilian and military accounts bear this out: the transition went smoothly as Union troops relieved Confederate guards of their supplies.

That same day, May 10, the Confederates camped around Meridian began to receive their paroles. Brigadier General George L. Andrews, Canby's provost marshal, oversaw the process.

At Meridian, 11,849 soldiers were paroled, along with 18,076 at Columbus and Gainesville, 6,304 in Jackson, 633 in Demopolis, and others in smaller numbers at more scattered locations. The total included in Taylor's surrender was 40,007. As at Bennett Place, this surrender was larger than the one at Appomattox. The two forces were also widely separated, as in North Carolina.

The spirit of cooperation between both sides was impressive. Federal orders stated that "the troops sent to garrison the posts in the interior, relieving troops of Lieutenant General Taylor's command, will be selected from those that are best disciplined and under charge of intelligent and discreet officers." Canby told Taylor to direct the placement of the Federal troops once they arrived at the Confederate camps. Taylor admitted the level of trust seemed strange to him, but "I delicately made some suggestions to these officers, which were adopted."

Over the next few weeks Taylor and Canby communicated by telegraph about the placement of Union troops and the paroling and transportation of Confederate soldiers going home. Orders also went to Union commanders in the region that said paroled soldiers of Lee's, Johnston's, and Taylor's armies were not to be disturbed, but any other confederate soldiers in arms were to be taken prisoner

After all the Confederate troops had departed from Meridian, Taylor went to Mobile, where Canby personally arranged for a horse to get him to New Orleans. Taylor was grateful, noting he had no personal resources, "else I must have begged my way."

In his farewell address to his troops, Taylor noted that he secured "terms for my troops as would preserve their honor and best protect them." Furthermore, he said, "All was conceded that I demanded. I demanded all that was necessary or proper."

"I DEMANDED ALL THAT WAS NECESSARY OR PROPER."

— LT. GEN. RICHARD TAYLOR

*   *   *

Lt. Gen. Nathan Bedford Forrest remains one of the best-known officers of the Confederacy for his fierce exploits, but his surrender in Gainesville was quiet and understated. (loc)

On May 9, the Confederate naval vessels at Nanna Hubba Bluff in northeastern Mobile County lowered their flags and turned over their ships and stores to Commander Edward Simpson of the Union's West Gulf Squadron. This important shipyard and supply base sat north of Mobile near Calvert. Twenty vessels were surrendered, though they were later used to return Union troops to Mobile from the interior of Alabama. "It was a splendid sight to witness those prize steamers coming down in line together," one Union soldier noted. "They were quite forlorn-looking—emblematic of the so-called Confederacy." Among them were the C.S.S. *Nashville*, C.S.S. *Baltic*, and C.S.S. *Morgan*.

The Citronelle surrender impacted the scattered troops of the Department of Alabama, Mississippi, and East Louisiana. Along the Big Black River in Mississippi near Yazoo City, the 3rd Texas Cavalry crossed into Union lines on May 5. They moved onto Vicksburg and camped, waiting for transports to take them home. Wrote one trooper of the situation, "All were satisfied."

Lieutenant General Nathan Bedford Forrest's cavalry had concentrated in Gainesville, Alabama, north of most of Taylor's troops. As they fell under the terms of the department's surrender, he disbanded his troopers on May 9. The men of the 7th Tennessee Cavalry cut up their regimental flag the night before they left. It was made from a wedding dress from a young woman. "The ceremony of tearing up the flag, fashioned from the bridal dress of an Aberdeen lady, was gone through with," Pvt. John Milton Hubbard noted, "and small bits

In Gainesville, two monuments commemorate the surrender and farewell speech of Nathan Bedford Forrest in a small park off Route 39. (bd)

of it distributed among the soldiers and officers of the Seventh Tennessee Regiment."

Brigadier General Ellias S. Dennis, who had commanded Illinois troops in various campaigns in Tennessee, Mississippi, and Louisiana, arrived to parole them with passes printed in Mobile. Naturally, the men had become bored and restless, holding horse and foot races, gambling, and seeking other diversions. Interactions with the arriving Union troops went smoothly, and Private Hubbard recalled, "at Macon, Miss., we drew our rations, which were bountiful as if there was no need of economy, and we had a long road before us."

In Meridian, General Maury addressed his remaining troops. "We shall lay down the arms which we have borne for four years to defend our rights—to win our liberties," he told them.

We have borne them with honor, and we only now surrender to the overwhelming power of the enemy, which has rendered further resistance hopeless and mischievous to our own people and cause. But we shall never forget the noble comrades who have stood shoulder to shoulder with us until now, the noble dead who have been martyred, the noble Southern women who have been wronged and are unavenged, or the noble principles for which we have fought.

"That we are beaten is a self-evident fact, and any further resistance on our part would justly be regarded as the very height of folly and rashness," Forrest told his troops. They were, he said, "the last of all the troops of the Confederate States Army east of the Mississippi River to lay down your arms." (bd)

Private Isaac Elliott of the 33rd Illinois wrote, "We remained at Greenville on the 22nd, where Gen. Grierson with his cavalry overtook us, bringing the official news of Lee's surrender. There was great rejoicing among the troops, and a salute was fired by the batteries."

On May 25, he noted that they arrived at Montgomery, and

marched into that beautiful city and saw the National Flag waving from the first capitol of the Confederacy. This building was an attractive place for the Union soldiers, and they thronged through it every day of our stay. They organized a Congress in the Assembly rooms, with delegates from every command in the corps; elected a President pro tern of the Senate, and a Speaker of the House, and formally abolished the Ordinance of Secession passed by the first Confederate Congress. Tried Jefferson Davis for high treason, and sentenced him to be hung; passed a law increasing the pay of the private soldier to $100.00 per month, and changed the army rations from hard bread *and salt pork to roast beef, turkey with cranberry sauce, oysters and pie. War was formally declared against England and France and an expedition organized to drive Maximilian out of Mexico, of which a private in the 33rd Illinois was given chief command.*

Major David W. Reed of the 12th Iowa noticed that paroled men from the Army of Northern Virginia began arriving soon after they marched into Montgomery: "They were without money, food, or clothing and came, in large numbers, into our camps, where the boys gladly shared rations with them."

*   *   *

Montgomery had been in turmoil for most of May. "On Monday, May 1st, sixteen days after the occurrence, Gen. Canby issued the official announcement of the assassination of President Lincoln," Isaac Elliot explained; "flags were placed at half mast, and half-hour guns fired through-out the day." Major Reed noted that upon getting the news, "A dead silence followed the reading for a few moments until the full import of the horrible crime was realized."

On May 4, news arrived of Johnston's surrender, and several days later news of Citronelle followed. Immediately the mission of the Union troops changed from one of seeking the enemy and destroying facilities to paroling enemy soldiers and peacekeeping.

Gainesville, now quiet and nearly forgotten, was once a busy river town. (bd)

After receiving orders to move towards the Confederate positions at Demopolis and Meridian, Isaac Elliot of the 33rd Illinois noted, "At 5:00 a. m. on the 10th our division started west, the 33rd in advance, and moved eight miles, passing through the beautiful little village of Prattville, where there was a cotton factory." At Demopolis on May 12 he observed, "a Mr. Todd, a Confederate officer, attracted considerable attention; he was a brother of Mrs. Abraham Lincoln."

They finally arrived at Meridian and, "our camp was moved a short distance and made quite pleasant among the large pine trees, headquarters being in a log house near by. We were destined to stay in this place for a long time, but a statement of our life and services from day to day will be unnecessary, as they were altogether uneventful."

The men were restless and became bored with their

duty now that active fighting was over. Elliott recorded that they spent their time on guard duty, loading trains with supplies bound for Mobile, and frequent drills. There was some break from the monotony, as Elliot noted: "A tribe of Choctaw Indians came from their reservation and camped close by and sold blackberries to the soldiers. They gave a war dance and exhibitions of Indian ball playing."

Later that summer, "A grand celebration of the Fourth of July was held in camp, where speeches were made by the members of the regiment, and Capt. Lewis read the Declaration of Independence. The barbaric Fugitive Slave Law had gone, the Emancipation Proclamation had been issued, and the Declaration now seemed to mean something."

General Taylor wrote his memoirs after the war and was active in the Democratic Party. He died in New York on April 12, 1879, and was buried in Metairie, Louisiana. General Nathan Bedford Forrest said of him, "He's the biggest man in the lot."

General Canby remained in the U.S. Army after the war and was killed while trying to reach a peace agreement with the Modoc Indians of California. He was shot, and his throat was cut by Modoc chiefs on April 11, 1873, in northern California. His body was returned home for burial in Indianapolis, Indiana.

The surrender in Alabama shared some similarities to that in North Carolina. Both forces were physically separated, both commanders met at a neutral site between their lines, and the surrender had to be negotiated twice due to changing conditions.

Yet this surrender lacked the widespread chaos and disorder seen at Greensboro. This is also the only surrender in which the Federal commander came prepared with food for the negotiators and a sizeable escort of troops. In Alabama the commanders also dealt with naval matters, something not covered in the two earlier surrenders.

Lastly, even though negotiations were agreed on, and had to be re-done, as in North Carolina, here it was done at two separate locations—the Magee house and the Burton house. The Alabama surrender also stands out because it took place at the only surviving original home—the Magee house—which remains on its original location and with its original furniture intact.

TEXAS

BATTLE OF PALMITO RANCH

THE LAST LAND ENGAGEMENT OF THE CIVIL WAR WAS FOUGHT NEAR THIS SITE ON MAY 12-13, 1865, THIRTY-FOUR DAYS AFTER ROBERT E. LEE SURRENDERED AT APPOMATTOX.

COL. THEODORE H. BARRETT COMMANDED FEDERAL TROOPS ON BRAZOS ISLAND 12 MILES TO THE EAST. THE CONFEDERATES OCCUPIED FORT BROWN 12 MILES TO THE WEST, COMMANDED BY GEN. JAMES E. SLAUGHTER AND COL. JOHN S. (RIP) FORD, WHOSE TROOPS HAD CAPTURED FORT BROWN FROM THE FEDERALS IN 1864.

ORDERED TO RECAPTURE THE FORT, LT. COL. DAVID BRANSON AND 300 MEN ADVANCED FROM BRAZOS ISLAND. THEY WON A SKIRMISH WITH CONFEDERATE PICKETS ON MAY 12. BARRETT REINFORCED BRANSON'S TROOPS WITH 200 MEN ON MAY 13 AND RENEWED THE MARCH TO FORT BROWN. CONFEDERATE CAVALRY HELD THE FEDERALS IN CHECK UNTIL FORD ARRIVED WITH REINFORCEMENTS THAT AFTERNOON. FORD'S ARTILLERY ADVANCED AND FIRED ON THE NORTHERN END OF THE FEDERAL LINE WHILE THE CAVALRY CHARGED. THE CONFEDERATE RIGHT CHARGED THE SOUTHERN END OF THE FEDERAL LINE AND CAPTURED PART OF THE UNION INFANTRY. BARRETT ORDERED A RETREAT TOWARD THE U.S. POSITION ON BRAZOS ISLAND.

WHILE THE CONFEDERATES REPORTED NO FATALITIES IN THE BATTLE OF PALMITO RANCH, THE UNION FORCES REPORTED FOUR OFFICERS AND 111 MEN KILLED, WOUNDED, OR MISSING.

(1989, 1990)

Chaos in the Trans-Mississippi

CHAPTER TWELVE
APRIL 14-MAY 15, 1865

While events unfolded in the east, troops in the vast Trans-Mississippi Department soldiered on. This area—geographically the largest military department of the Confederacy—included modern-day Arkansas, Missouri, Oklahoma (known as Indian Territory), Texas, and Louisiana west of the Mississippi. Despite the size of his realm, though, department commander Lt. Gen. Edmund Kirby Smith was an unhappy man.

A native of Florida, Smith had attended West Point as part of the class of 1845 and taught there afterward. He fought in the Mexican war and rose to the rank of major in the U.S. Army before resigning to join the Confederate military.

Now nestled at departmental headquarters in Shreveport, Louisiana, he felt abandoned by his government and betrayed by his subordinates—and his men were getting unhappier by the day, too.

Governor Henry Watkins Allan, also situated there, did his best to manage the state's affairs, provide for its citizens, and keep the economy and war effort going. Under his administration, salt works, clothing depots, distilleries, turpentine production, and cotton processing all increased.

On February 18, local citizens witnessed a review and a mock battle. "Some fair ladies screamed," reported one witness, and afterwards the troops and guests "repaired to tables, where a bountiful and substantial repast was spread."

But such displays, intended to improve morale,

Even as the Confederacy collapsed, Confederate forces scored a victory in the last fight of the war. In the battle of Palmito Ranch—also spelled "Palmetto"—Federal Col. Theodore H. Barrett's 500 men picked a fight with Confederates on May 12, and a day later, Col. John S. "Rip" Ford's 300 Confederates finished it. Federals sustained 118 casualties compared to six Confederates. (hmdb.org/rem)

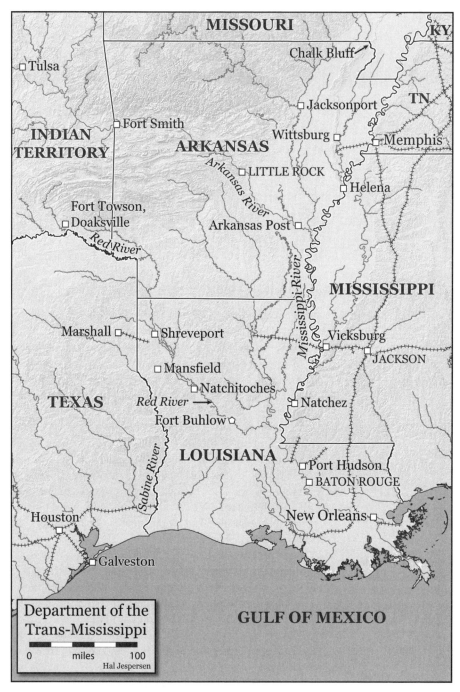

DEPARTMENT OF THE TRANS-MISSISSIPPI—The events related to the surrender of the Trans-Mississippi Department took place over a wide area. The bulk of the Confederate forces were in Shreveport, Louisiana, when surrender negotiations began, but pockets of troops were scattered well west into Texas and north into Arkansas, as well as in Indian Territory.

were smoke and mirrors. Supplies were growing more difficult to procure for the embattled army commander. In March, Smith started a furlough system—in part to improve conditions and in part to alleviate pressure on supplies—allowing 10% of a unit to visit home at a time. He also initiated efforts to improve rations.

But tension was building in the ranks. Both actions calmed, but did not reverse, the dissention and desertion. The men had not been paid and were restless. Price increases put basic necessities out of reach for soldiers and civilians. "Confederate money was almost worthless," noted Maj. Silas Grisamore of the 18th Louisiana. "A country man brought in ten chickens, which brought him one hundred dollars, and they would have been sold ten times later for three-times that amount. Desertions began to become frequent; the men, seeing no future prospect before them, deliberately went to their homes."

A trooper in the 2nd Louisiana Cavalry noted, "Missouri and Ark. troops are deserting daily and going home to fight no more. Every night as many as 6 and sometimes 12 soldiers desert from the Infantry and go home or with the Yankees." Desertion was so rampant that, in the Confederate camps near Alexandria, executions for deserters were held every Friday. One failed mutiny resulted in 35 executions.

"The Armey hear is very much demoralized," wrote Pvt. Henry Morgan of the 31st Louisiana, camped near Alexandria, in a letter to his wife. A subsequent letter noted, "The boys is praying . . . in camps and wee see them nelt don all about in the woods praying for pease."

And it was no wonder, as Grisamore noted that the troops from Virginia, North Carolina, and Alabama were "returning by hundreds into Louisiana and Texas, rendering the facts certain that the war was rapidly drawing to a close and that it would be futile for the Trans-Mississippi Department to attempt to remain in the field."

Major General Harry T. Hays wrote to another officer, "I am mortified to have to tell you that my own division, though at much greater distance from the enemy than your command, are becoming—have become— disgracefully demoralized. Last night one hundred & fifty men, mostly from the 29th Regt left in a body with their arms in their hands."

Kirby Smith appealed to Richmond for money to pay his men, noting that his department "was practically without funds and without the means of procuring

Commanding the Trans-Mississippi Department, Lt. Gen. Edmund Kirby Smith's hand was forced into surrender by his troops and subordinate officers. (loc)

them." Civilians were increasingly unwilling to accept government credit for goods.

Smith's appeals went unanswered, though. The government in the east was on the run, although Smith had no way of knowing it.

*   *   *

On April 14—nearly a week after Appomattox, and the day Lincoln would be assassinated—Lt. W. P. Renwick of the 3rd Louisiana wrote to his wife. "I firmly believe that we will yet achieve our independence," he optimistically opined.

That very day, however, Smith announced to the soldiers in his department that Lee had surrendered—yet all was not lost, he believed.

"With you rests the hopes of our nation, and upon your action depends the fate of our people," Smith wrote. He went on, invoking them to "prove to the world that your hearts have not failed in the hour of disaster" and instructing them to "sustain the holy cause." He noted that the department still had "the means of long-resisting invasion. The great resources of this department, its vast extent, the numbers, the discipline, and the efficiency of the army" will secure "the final success of our cause."

Built in the Navy yard in Shreveport's Cross Bayou, at the mouth of the Red River, the C.S.S. *Missouri* had been stranded by low water since its construction. Finally freed in March of 1865, the ship would see limited service until its surrender on June 3. It was the last Confederate ironclad to surrender. (ecw)

Smith gave an inspirational address to the men, yet the mood in the ranks was gloomy. "The men instantly became dejected," admitted Pvt. C. S. Bell. "Mutiny and wholesale desertion was openly talked of. This soon gave way to a general feeling of apathy and indifference."

On April 19, Maj. Gen. John Pope, commanding the Union's Division of the Mississippi, called on Smith to surrender his department and enclosed details of the meeting between Lee and Grant in Virginia. Colonel John T. Sprague left St. Louis with the communication and met Confederate officers at the mouth of the Red River who escorted him to Shreveport. Sprague had specific instructions to only offer the same terms as Appomattox, and "not commit the Government to any policy." Upon arriving in Shreveport, Sprague delivered his information to Smith.

However, a public meeting in Shreveport on April 26—the day Johnston and Sherman agreed to final terms—saw several speeches confirm the conviction to fight on. "A great amount of patriotism and valor were let off in the shape of eloquent speeches," said one eyewitness. Several high-ranking Confederate officers secretly discussed arresting Smith should he surrender the department, and they made plans to move their loyal troops in to seize supplies and arrest government officials who cooperated with Smith.

This proved unnecessary. Smith was discussing plans to send an envoy to Havana, where it was thought Jefferson Davis had fled to, and bring him to the Trans-Mississippi to continue the war. Smith was also sending an emissary to Mexico with the hope of forming an alliance. On May 9, he wrote to the governors of Texas, Arkansas, and Missouri that his forces were still strong and, despite the "disparity of numbers" with the enemy, his army had "valor and skill." He then requested a meeting with the governors to discuss future actions.

As he awaited their responses, Smith turned his attention back to Colonel Sprague, still waiting at Shreveport. The "propositions for the surrender of the troops under my command," Smith said, "are not such that my sense of duty and honor will permit me to accept."

*   *   *

Even as Smith tried to figure out his next move, conditions in Shreveport continued to deteriorate. Robberies and desertion were increasing. Smith and his staff did not go out at night as it was too dangerous.

On May 10 near Natchitoches, midway between Shreveport and Alexandria, Maj. Gen. Simon B. Buckner reviewed the units. Colonel Winchester Hall of the 26th Louisiana noted that Buckner, "with head uncovered, and his long hair given to the wind, rode rapidly down the line followed by his staff."

Yet, Hall noted, "In spite of the vigilance of the officers, the picketing of roads, the doubling of camp guards, and other precautions, desertions were now becoming numerous among those who considered further contention useless." Furthermore, he observed, "each squad of deserters left us with less means to keep together, or to make a lengthy march."

That same day in Opelousas, 50 miles west of New

The scrublands along the Rio Grande outside Brownsville, Texas, provided a harsh backdrop for the war's final fight, the battle of Palmito Ranch. (hmdb.org/rem)

Orleans, Sgt. Edwin Foy of the 7th Louisiana Cavalry wrote that news of Taylor's surrender on the 4th reached them. In a letter, he told his wife he was going to Brazil with others.

To the southwest, on May 12, the last land battle was fought at Palmito Ranch, Texas. In a badly coordinated operation, Union forces were scattered and defeated by Texas troops along the Rio Grande.

* * *

On May 13, in Marshall, Texas, the governors of Texas, Arkansas, Louisiana, and Missouri responded to Smith's request for advice. They told him to "disband his armies in the department; officers and men to return immediately to their former homes or such as they may select . . . and there to remain as good citizens, freed from all disabilities, and restored to all the rights of citizenship."

They also put forth five proposals, including that Union authorities grant immunity from prosecution to soldiers and citizens, and that present state governments be allowed to function.

Thus, when Smith turned his attention to Colonel Sprague on May 15, he did so believing he was operating from a position of relative strength. After telling Sprague he could not accept the terms offered by the Federals, Smith shared the proposals of the governors, which called for an end to the war, "provided certain measures which they deem necessary to the public order and proper security of the people" were met by the Union government. Smith furthermore stated that his army was "well appointed and supplied, not immediately threatened, and with its communications open."

Smith admitted that "[i]t is not contended that the Trans-Mississippi Department can without assistance accomplish its independence against the whole power of the United States." Yet he maintained that they would only be defeated "after great and expensive preparations."

Thus, he explained the terms that he and the governors would accept from a position of strength. "Many examples in history teach that the more generous the terms proposed by a victorious enemy the greater the certainty of a speedy and lasting pacification," he concluded.

Sprague then went downriver to report at New Orleans.

Galveston Harbor

CHAPTER THIRTEEN

MAY-JUNE 1865

In Virginia, one general surrendered; in North Carolina, one disobeyed orders to surrender; in Alabama, one chose surrender.

In the Trans-Mississippi, Edmund Kirby Smith had the decision made for him.

"All kinds of rumors, and excitement intense," Sgt. W. W. Heartsill of the 2nd Texas Cavalry wrote in his diary at Shreveport on May 15. "The men can be seen in squads and crowds, talking and speculating over the news, some are rejoicing to think the war is so near over, while others would rather see it last years upon years."

Things continued to go downhill. A Shreveport citizen noted that "clouds thicken around us from every quarter, every countenance is filled with despondency." In the camps around Shreveport, wild rumors circulated that both confirmed and denied an imminent surrender. This was the final straw, and men began to break into commissary stores and leave camp in droves. One soldier recalled that the men "gathered in groups everywhere . . . both officers and men, swore fearful oaths never to surrender. The humiliation was unbearable."

By May 13, the situation was so volatile that the few loyal remaining quartermasters officers began loading supplies to transfer them west to Texas for safety. Said one observer, "Troops began to leave for home, openly and unmolested."

That same day in Alexandria, Adjutant D. F. Boyd of the 7th Louisiana Cavalry wrote, "All is confusion and demoralization here, nothing like order and discipline

Despite a solid performance delaying Federals during the 1862 Peninsula Campaign in Virginia, Maj. Gen. John B. Magruder ran afoul of Robert E. Lee. Already under orders to transfer west, Magruder complied and, in Texas, again demonstrated capable command. In 1863, he successfully defended Galveston from Federals. Despite that, he found himself in 1865 helping to oversee the surrender of the Trans-Mississippi there. The Virginia-born Magruder remained in Galveston after the war and, after his death in 1871, was buried there in the Episcopal Cemetery. (pg)

Confederate cannon lined up in Baton Rouge after the surrender. (cphcw)

remains. Heavy desertions and plundering of Government property of every kind is the order of the day."

Three days later, Col. Winchester Hall of the 26th Louisiana noted, "rumors were in circulation in camp that Shreveport would be set on fire that night and plundered."

The 3rd Louisiana, which had few desertions up to this point, learned of rumors that they were to be relieved by Missouri troops since other Louisianans were deserting. On May 18, a Missouri Regiment surrounded them, and overnight, insulted by being guarded, many of the Pelican-state troops departed. Governor Allen then arrived to address them, but it was no use. "What a torturing reality," Hall admitted.

On May 17, the troops of General Hays' division moved from Natchitoches to Mansfield. "The Division became a mob and rabble," Colonel Richardson noted, "disregarding the authority of their superiors and governed alone by a spirit of lawless plunder and pillage. Predatory bands were formed."

The 26th and 28th Louisiana were sent to Mansfield to stop looting and restore order. The troops arrived to find the storehouses already pillaged. They gathered around the flagpole and lowered the colors while the regimental band played a solemn song. Colonel Winchester Hall of the 26th Louisiana observed, "While the band played a dirge it was torn to pieces, and a piece given to each member as a memento." Hall wrote that he broke the staff and burned it.

The regiments then marched home, maintaining their organization and discipline, until the men, as Hall noted, "one by one dropped out of the ranks, as they reached their respective dwellings." Hall wrote, "I continued with them until we came to a place where our routes were in different directions. I stood in the road, and shook hands with each one as they filed by me saying, 'Vous avez bein fait votre devoir.'"

And so it went. The army literally began to dissolve. Major Grisamore of the 18th Louisiana noted:

No sooner were we camped on the Lower Shreveport road, than the fact became apparent that the war was concluded and that a grand tableau of dissolving views was about to be exhibited without any admission fees. The next day information came to me that my quarters were to be overhauled by the troops and the mules and wagons were to be appropriated by them. What was to be done in order to save my baggage and that of the dozen detailed men who were with me was the greatest question to be decided by us.

After meeting with his staff, they removed

one of the wheels off each of two wagons and sunk them in the little bayou on which we were encamped. This bright idea was originated that some of our horses and mules might be hid in the woods until we were ready to start, and a teamster, residing in Mansfield, named Clark, told me privately that he knew all the ravines of the country and that if I would give him a mule, he would show the boys where to conceal theirs so than nobody could find them.

Grisamore continues, "Clark fulfilled his promise, and then went to his home in Mansfield and had the gratification of learning, the next morning, that his mule had been stolen out of his stable. Major Wedge, our commissary, sent his team into the woods, and the next day his horse was sent into camp with the information that his 'trusty friend,' who had been sent out in charge, had gone with his mule." Grisamore concludes the story noting, "The last I saw of the major, he was following his wagon, drawn by hired oxen, with a countenance as long as a text in moral law."

Major Grisamore had a personal encounter with the looting:

I managed to save mules enough to transport the papers and baggage of the colonel and his aide-de-camp. I had a box of clothing and some stationary that I was intending to distribute as soon as we got into camp and was preparing to make a distribution when about a dozen fellows came up and expressed an anxious desire to see into the box. As I had all my own papers and baggage in another wagon, I was peculiarly solicitous to attract their attention from it and became quite spunky, telling them that they should not see into the box and that it was none of their business what was in it, etc. Gathering around the wagon like a gang of hungry wolves, preparatory to a charge, I got myself in a good position, and after a good deal of talking, I turned my head, when they pitched into the box and began relieving it of its contents. I threw about half the articles over my head into the hands of my detailed men, who took good care of them.

By May 19, most of the Louisiana troops had gone, taking government horses, mules, and wagons. They had been issued clothes, linen, cotton, thread, buttons, and leather, from the quartermaster, and used these items to barter on their way home. "Notwithstanding the universal pillage of the departing soldiers," Grisamore conceded, "I have always commended them for one generous trait. Not a private horse was taken, nor a trunk or anything that was not government property."

On May 20, those remaining were furloughed and allowed to go. Moving downriver on pontoons, or walking the dirt roads, they said their goodbyes and turned away from Shreveport.

Mansfield saw a great many of the Louisiana troops depart for home starting on May 19 and continuing for the next few days. The 17th Louisiana disbanded, but Company C remained to guard ammunition. The 18th Louisiana Consolidated—consisting of the 18th Regiment and 10th Battalion—and the 28th and 29th Regiments all disbanded. The Texas troops, stationed in Hempstead and elsewhere, began to disband, too.

Grisamore noted the lawlessness of the region. "We were so few that we did not dare go to Natchitoches alone," he wrote, "and were not certain of finding our friends there if we did. . . . For two days, the men of north Louisiana had been leaving . . ." Instead, he and his comrades made their way home, 400 miles away, with the mules and wagons they managed to keep from the hands of thieves. They received some corn and bacon from Confederate commissary depots to get them through.

All across northern and western Louisiana, thousands of men were on the road, headed for home.

* * *

By May 18, things in Shreveport had deteriorated so much that Smith left by stagecoach for Houston to

LEFT: John Magruder was known as "Prince John" because he loved to stage amateur theater productions. RIGHT: In early 1862, Simon Buckner had been left holding the bag at Ft. Donelson, where he was forced to surrender the fort and its army to his old friend, Ulysses S. Grant. In the spring of 1865, Buckner found himself holding the bag again for another surrender even as his superior, Kirby Smith, vanished into Texas with plans to rally the Confederacy from there. Magruder would help Buckner with the arrangements. (loc)

move his headquarters there, a safer location farther from possible Union attack—though it was internal strife that was gradually destroying his army. Smith left Gen. Simon B. Buckner in charge while he relocated.

Smith had, in the meanwhile, been receiving reports from Maj. Gen. John B. Magruder that forces in Texas were also disintegrating. On May 14, troops in Galveston had mutinied when nearly 400 of them tried to march off. Magruder sent two loyal regiments to stop them. The mutiny ended without bloodshed but the message was clear: the troops were unwilling to serve any longer.

Smith hoped to reorganize in Texas now that most of his Louisiana troops had left. His intention was to move all of the troops to Texas, either to keep fighting or to move on to Mexico. En route, he wrote that he felt "abandoned and mortified, left without either men or material, I feel powerless to do good for my country." He hoped that the Union government would be conciliatory toward the South.

Far away in Washington, that Union government was reveling in its victory. The Army of the Potomac marched in the Grand Review on May 23, followed by the veterans of the Army of the Tennessee the next day. For much of the north, the celebration of the war's end was in full swing. Regiments were returning to their home states to muster out of service and men would be on their way home.

*   *   *

After Smith's departure from Shreveport, the remaining troops, largely from Arkansas and Missouri, also began to desert in droves. "The men looked upon the Government property as abandoned, and sought to appropriate whatever could be found," said Colonel Hall of the 26th Louisiana. When he asked for volunteers from the 26th to step forward and guard it, "The call was without a response." Hall noted, though, that "officers of the division were steadfast to the bitter end."

That day the commissary stores in the camps were pillaged, and with organization breaking down, officers couldn't maintain control. Colonel R. Richardson, commanding Hays' Division, instructed commanders to "temporarily disband and permit them to proceed to their homes, there to await further orders."

However, on May 21, full-scale looting broke out in Shreveport, with troops and civilians rushing stores and commissary depots. Again, Missouri troops arrived to restore order. In the camps around the town, Pvt. James A. Small of the 17th Louisiana noted that many soldiers had bent their rifle barrels around trees or driven their bayonets into the ground, "swearing they were going back home regardless of the consequences." Another wrote, "It was awful, terrible beyond portrayal."

General Bucker, in camp near Mansfield, saw similar disarray. On May 19, he addressed his troops, sounding much the same note Richardson had in Shreveport:

The major portion of the command having deserted camp and gone to their homes, all the government animals and most of the wagons having been forcibly taken possession of and carried away, the Commissary and Quartermaster's Departments of this command and the Post at Mansfield having been pillaged by the troops; all completely paralyzing the present military organization, and rendering the maintaining of discipline and the subsistence of the troops any longer impossible, brigade commanders are hereby authorized to temporarily disband the troops under their command, and to permit them to proceed to their homes, there to await further orders from their commanding officers.

Of course everyone knew there would be no further orders: their war was ending.

The breakdown in order at Mansfield and Shreveport, happening while Smith was away, influenced the decision of the generals and governors to end the war. Major General Harry Hays, commanding the Department of West Louisiana, issued orders:

The major portion of this command having deserted camp and gone to their homes, all the Government animals and most of the wagons having been forcibly

*taken possession of and carried away, the quartermaster's
and commissary departments of this command and the
post at Mansfield having been pillaged by the troops, all
completely paralyzing the present military organizations,
and rendering the maintaining of discipline and
subsistence of the troops longer impossible, brigade
commanders are hereby authorized to disband the troops
under their commands and to permit them to proceed
to their homes, there to await further orders from their
commanding officers.*

Those orders, of course, never came. The troops
were going home, even before the surrender was signed.

*   *   *

By now the breakdown had spread to the garrisons
in Texas. In Houston, Austin, and San Antonio, shops
were looted, supplies were stolen from government
warehouses, and organized troops left their posts. D. W.
C. Bates of the *Austin Intelligencer* reported,

*Company after Company of men came to the place, and
the idea having occurred . . . that there was large amount
of quartermaster and commissary stores stored in
various parts of the city . . . The scene beggars
description. Crowds of soldiers collected in front of
every government building in town, demanding the
keys, and when they were not forthcoming, a forcible
entrance was made and the grab game commenced.
The mania to "hold fast what you can get and
catch what you can" was not confined to soldiers.
Numbers of men who had never taken part in the
fighting . . . together with women, children, and
Negros, assembled around the places where coffee, flour,
sugar, salt, bacon, cloth, rope, leather, cotton, etc. were
dealt out with unsparing hand.*

Camp Ford, the largest
Confederate prisoner of war
camp in the Trans-Mississippi,
was located in Tyler, Texas.
The camp closed on May
19, 1865, as the wave of
surrenders swept across the
Lone Star State. (ecw)

In Austin, George Freeman was a discharged soldier
who organized a volunteer militia force to help maintain
order during the chaos. When he heard rumors that
robbers were going to seize the unguarded state treasury,
he gathered 30 followers and moved on the Treasury
building, near the state capitol. Arriving at dark, they
heard the sound of sledgehammers at work inside the
building. Freeman's men fired and the estimated 30-40
robbers inside returned fire, wounding Freeman. "There
was simply a volley from perhaps half a dozen rifles and
the groans of a single wounded man."

The thieves made off with about $65,000 in gold and silver, but left behind much more in U.S. bonds, coupons, and securities, as well as $3 million dollars in Confederate and Texas bank notes. Freeman and his follower occupied the Treasury and guarded it until Union forces arrived in late July. They were later thanked by the Texas legislature, but never paid. Afterwards Freeman became a lawyer and helped endow Baylor University. He died in 1910.

Texas cavalryman Sgt. W. W. Heartsill noted that 75 men left one night from the 19th Louisiana and 30 from the 12th. On May 20, his unit marched to Sterling, where they learned that they were to disband; they also learned they were allowed to take company wagons to their county and stay armed to protect themselves. "Soldiers of the First Texas Cavalry Brigade, you are now once more citizens of Texas," said one officer. "Farewell."

In east Texas, Marshall was an important site for the Confederacy's war effort. It was the headquarters for the Trans-Mississippi Department's Medical Bureau and Postal Service. It also had a powder mill, hat factory, arsenal, supply depot, and ordnance bureau. Marshall was the capital for the pro-Confederate government of Missouri that had gone into exile from November 1863 onward. Three wartime conferences took place there between governors and military officers from Texas, Arkansas, Louisiana, and Missouri.

In Marshall, Gens. Jo Shelby, Simon B. Buckner, William B. Preston, and John G. Walker gathered from their scattered commands to discuss the situation. They elected Buckner to proceed to New Orleans and surrender on behalf of Smith. Meanwhile, Magruder and Texas Governor Murrah, coming together in Shreveport from Texas, authorized Col. Asbel Smith and a citizen named W. P. Ballinger to proceed to New Orleans to also negotiate a surrender. They received a pass from Admiral Thatcher and moved down the Red River on the *U.S.S. Antonia*.

Buckner arrived first. On May 26, he, Maj. Gen. Sterling Price, and Maj. Gen. Joseph L. Brent arrived at Baton Rouge then proceeded on to New Orleans. At the St. Charles Hotel, Buckner met with Union Maj. Gen. Peter Osterhaus, representing Canby.

The St. Charles Hotel was a prominent New Orleans landmark. Actually the second hotel on the site, it was originally constructed in 1837, and rebuilt following an 1851 fire. The hotel had famously refused service to

A former governor of Missouri, Mag. Gen. Sterling Price, known by his men as "Old Pap," fled with his remaining troops to Mexico rather than surrender. He unsuccessfully sought service with Emperor Maximillian and was forced to return to Missouri, where he died destitute. (loc)

Union Gen. Benjamin F. Butler, the head of occupation forces, in 1862. Butler responded by having the business closed and took over the hotel by force.

Subsequently, the hotel had additional fires in 1876, 1880, and 1894. The last hotel, built in 1895 in the Beaux Arts style, was torn down in 1974.

Buckner had been the first to surrender an army earlier in the war, at Ft. Donelson in 1862. Now, since he was not the Trans-Mississippi Department's commander, he had to produce proof for Osterhaus that he had the authority to act in Smith's stead. Upon showing orders that he was given authority in Smith's absence, negotiations got underway. Representing the Confederate naval forces was Captain Carter.

Buckner and Carter proposed to surrender their forces based on the same terms granted at Appomattox and Bennett Place. These were the only terms Union commanders were authorized to accept, so there was little to discuss. According to a newspaper article, the interview "was a pleasant one." There are no other details of the meeting known, other than it was held about midday. The steamer *Fort Jackson* rushed to Galveston with copies of the terms.

The site of the St. Charles Hotel is now a parking lot. No markers exist denoting the opening negotiations to surrender the Confederacy's largest military department. (ono)

Buckner then returned to Shreveport where he reorganized the remaining Missouri troops. A select group of 1,000 received new uniforms, horses, and rifles. The men marched west into Texas. Their destination: Mexico. Other generals headed for the Rio Grande included Magruder, Price, Shelby, and Smith. Buckner hid a small silk Confederate flag under his coat, and proceeded with his wife and daughter to New Orleans to resume private life. The remaining soldiers at Shreveport were paroled and began returning home.

On May 27, Smith reached Houston, only to learn that his war was over. The day before, Buckner had surrendered the Trans-Mississippi Department on his behalf. Reluctantly he joined Magruder in Galveston where, on June 2, Smith formally surrendered on board the steamer *Fort Jackson* to Brig. Gen. Edmund Davis, representing Canby.

Ironically, the same day Smith went onboard the

The U.S.S. *Fort Jackson* saw service along the coast of the Carolinas until being transferred to the Gulf blockade squadron in February 1865. (cphcw)

Fort Jackson in Galveston harbor, a ship arrived bringing home the Texans from the Army of Northern Virginia who surrendered at Appomattox.

Galveston, like other communities in east Texas, had seen its fair share of unrest that spring. By June of 1865, its garrison included remnants of the 2nd, 8th, 20th, 21st Texas Infantry, 2nd Texas Cavalry, Bradford's Cavalry, Waul's Texas Legion, and the 1st Texas Heavy Artillery. There had been great unrest, and threats of rebellion among these troops. Many were unpaid and ready to leave their posts.

Smith gave his final address in Houston on May 30:

> *Soldiers—The day after I refused the demand of the Federal Government to surrender this department I left Shreveport for Houston. I ordered the Missouri, Arkansas, and Louisiana troops to follow. My purpose was to concentrate the entire strength of the department, await negotiation, and if possible, secure terms alike honorable to solders and citizens. Failing in this, I intended to struggle to the last, and with an army united in purpose, firm in resolve, and battling for the right, I believed God would yet give us the victory. I reached here to fid the Texas troops disbanded and hastening to their homes. They had forsaken their colors and their commanders, had abandoned the cause for which they were struggling, and appropriated the public property to their personal use.*
>
> *Soldiers, I am left a commander without an army—a general without troops. You have made your choice. It was unwise and unpatriotic, but it is final. I pray you may not live to regret it. The enemy will now possess your country and dictate his own laws. You have voluntarily destroyed our organization and thrown away all means of resistance. Your present duties are plain. Return to your families. Resume the occupations of peace. Yield obedience to the laws. Labor to restore order. Strive, both by counsel and example, to give security to life and property. And may God in his mercy direct you aright, and heal the wound of our distracted country.*
>
> *E. Kirby Smith, General*

About 15-17,000 troops—the remnants of the Trans-Mississippi Department—were left at the time. Most of these units were Arkansas, Missouri, and Texas troops, the Louisianans having largely deserted already. Very few got paroles. Typical were at the men of the Louisiana Heavy Artillery's 8th Battalion, stationed at Fort Buhlow near Pineville, Louisiana: they simply went home, not wanting their paroles. Union troops moved up to occupy the fort on June 2.

On June 3, Lt. Commander J. H. Carter surrendered the Confederate naval ships on the Red River at Alexandria to Commander W. E. Fitzhugh. Included in the transfer was the C.S.S. *Missouri*.

Union troops under Maj. Gen. Francis Herron began arriving in Shreveport on June 6. They immediately began to restore order, issue paroles, and clean up litter in the streets. Most of the Louisianans had gone, but about 15,000 men from Missouri and Kentucky remained in good order. Once paroled, the former Confederates were free to return home. The captured artillery was sent to New Orleans.

Following his surrender, Smith fled to Mexico, and then to Cuba, before returning to Virginia in November of 1865 to sign an amnesty oath. He was the last surviving full Confederate general, passing away in 1893.

Unfortunately, there is nothing in either Galveston or New Orleans to commemorate the events there. A marker in the Galveston Yacht Club (above) notes that the surrender occurred there, but gives no details. The locations of events have been lost, and no museums or historic sites are associated with the events of May 1865. (hmdb.org/je)

The End in Arkansas

CHAPTER FOURTEEN

MAY 11, 1865

Although included in the Trans-Mississippi Department, the Confederate troops in Arkansas made their own arrangements with local Union commanders to surrender. By 1864, the capital at Little Rock had been occupied and a Union government installed. Much of the upper and western part of Arkansas was under Union military control. However, in March 1865, Confederate Brig. Gen. Meriwether Jefferson Thompson had taken command of the Northern Sub-District of Arkansas. Several expeditions of Union troops entered northeastern Arkansas to seek him out and ask his surrender.

One of those expeditions was led by Lt. Col. Charles W. Davis, assistant provost marshal in St. Louis. He departed on April 30 with instructions that he should propose the same terms as at Appomattox, and "no other terms." In addition, "civil matters will not be treated or talked of."

Accompanied by Capt. J. F. Bennett, Davis picked up a cavalry escort, entered Arkansas, and moved down to Chalk Bluff, where the St. Francis River formed the Missouri/Arkansas border, arriving on May 4. Davis sent messengers out in search of Thompson, who agreed to meet.

Cut off from the rest of the department and facing potential attack from Union forces in several directions, Thompson felt compelled to discuss surrender. He and four officers arrived at Davis' camp at Chalk Bluff on May 9. Upon meeting Davis, he said he wanted to consult his brigade commanders, but agreed to remain at the Union camp. The Confederate commissioners stayed at the Liddle home near Chalk Bluff. There are no descriptions of the house or details of the family.

Although no battles were fought at Jacksonport, Arkansas, it was a troop mustering site and important supply base throughout the war. (jsp)

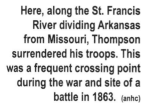

Here, along the St. Francis River dividing Arkansas from Missouri, Thompson surrendered his troops. This was a frequent crossing point during the war and site of a battle in 1863. (anhc)

Brig. Gen. Merriweather Jefferson Thompson achieved acclaim as almost a folk hero of the Trans-Mississippi. Known as the "Swamp Fox of the Confederacy" for his early war exploits in southeast Missouri, he also had a side-wheel river steamer in the Confederate Navy named after him. (loc)

Davis described his counterpart as "a witty fellow, and is continually talking about impossibilities. He has not decided to surrender yet. Shall try to convince him. If he gives up it will be hard to find his army."

Thompson asked Davis about specific details:

(1) Should my officers and men assemble at specified times and places? And will your army then have to pass over the country or simply move to the points designated to complete the surrender and parole the men?

(2) Will families of those who prefer to leave after being paroled be banished?

(3) Does the parole given Gen. Lee cover their private personal property—horses owned by soldiers, and private personal property at their home?

Davis responded that this army would not impact the countryside, but only move to the rendezvous points; that families would not be banished so long as they obeyed the laws; and that private property would be respected. Davis also provided a sample of an Appomattox parole so Thompson could see it for himself.

Thompson's last concern was those troops who had to travel from the region down to Texas or Louisiana, because as of that time, the Trans-Mississippi Department had not yet surrendered and no one knew if it would. Davis reassured him the former Confederates could return home undisturbed.

Satisfied, at 5:00 on the afternoon of May 11, Thompson returned to Davis' headquarters at Chalk Bluff. "Upon the promise you have made me that the U.S. forces will not necessarily move over the country," he said, "I have determined to accept the terms offered and will and hereby do surrender the forces under my

Jacksonport, photographed in 1875, just ten years after the surrender (jsp)

command upon the terms granted to Gen. Robert E. Lee and the Army of Northern Virginia, the officers and men of the Confederate States army now serving or being in the Northern Sub-District of Arkansas."

There are no accounts stating the details of the meeting: exactly where they met at Chalk Bluff, or the specifics of the conversation. Reports are unclear as to whether the officers met on the Arkansas or Missouri side of the river, though it seems clear Thompson and his staff were on the southern side, and Davis on the Missouri shore.

Davis proposed that the Confederate troops east of Cache River and White River south of the mouth of the Cache assemble at Wittsburg on May 25 to be paroled, and those west of the Cache and White and below the mouth of the Cache proceed to Jacksonport on June 5. To this Thompson agreed and issued orders to his scattered regiments. His command was widely dispersed throughout northeast Arkansas to better access forage and supplies.

Although Jacksonport is off the beaten path, the visitor who journeys there is rewarded with many historic markers. (jsp)

About a third refused to surrender, though, and instead deserted. Shelby's Missouri Brigade and members of Green's and Jackman's Missouri Brigades left for Mexico. Some Missouri units disbanded rather than surrender their colors. Many men simply went home.

Davis' party, along with one Confederate officer, proceeded to Memphis and then up the St. Francis River to Wittsburg. There they met up with Thompson, and on May 25, paroled about 2,000 Confederates.

Moving in from the west, the 3rd Minnesota occupied

Jacksonport and other sites along the river. Jacksonport had been a prosperous town before the war, its economy built on steamships. It was also a mustering point for many local units that organized at the war's start, and even during the course of the war. The 32nd Arkansas, for example, had been recruited at Jacksonport in May 1861 and surrendered here on June 5, 1865. Another example was the 47th Arkansas Cavalry, which began and ended its career there.

Some of the Arkansans were likely home to witness the surrender in their home county, while other local units were present at other surrenders. Thrall's Artillery Battery had been organized there, and the unit was part of Taylor's Citronelle surrender. The 38th Arkansas, organized in Jacksonport in 1862, found itself near Marshall, Texas, when the Trans-Mississippi Department was surrendered.

Jacksonsport was occupied by both sides at different times in the war, earning visits from important figures such as Gens. Stirling Price, Theophilus Holmes, Jo Shelby, Earl Van Dorn, Jeff Thompson, John S. Marmaduke, and Frederick Steele. (jsp)

While most of the men on the Jacksonport parole lists actually served in the unit with which they surrendered, some men had attached themselves to various regiments solely for the purpose of surrendering. A few probably never saw any service except marching with their relatives and neighbors to Jacksonport to receive the paroles, which were thought to provide the former Confederates with some degree of protection from later arrest.

Ultimately 1,964 enlisted men with 193 officers paroled at Wittsburg on May 25, and 4,854 enlisted men with 443 officers paroled at Jacksonport on June 5, for a grand total of 7,806.

Thompson, Davis, and their staffs all met in Jacksonport for the final surrender. An estimated 8,000 people—soldiers and civilians—crowded the town's waterfront. Thompson appeared, to one Union office, "a queer looking genius, dressed in a suit of snowy white from the plume in his hat to the heel of his boot, and with a sword belt and white gloves. He is a clever chap, full of fun, telling great yarns and an incessant talker."

Thompson's address, scathing, but not the only one critical of his men, was delivered from a steamship at Jacksonport. At one point a soldier called out, "General, talk to us like gentlemen." Another threatened that Thompson might be mobbed.

"Mob, hell," Thompson replied, "I don't scare damn." He then called "Attention," and his troops instantly stood straight and silent. "If you men don't stand still and listen to me, there are enough one-leg and one-arm men and sick soldiers with honorable discharges in their pockets among you to whip all the balance!"

One soldier called out, "Give 'em hell, General, they deserve it." "Go to it, General," said another. Thompson spoke with passion from the ship's upper deck:

Many of the 8000 men I now see around me, very many of you, have been skulking for the last three years in the swamps within a few miles of our own homes—skulking duty—and during that time have not seen your own children. I see many faces about me that have not been seen any mortal man for the last three years, and what have you been doing all that time? Why, you have been lying in the swamps until the moss has grown six inches long on your back, and such men call themselves "chivalrous soldiers." But you rally like brave and gallant men around Uncle Sam's commissary stores, and I now come to surrender you, and hope you will make better citizens than you have soldiers.

Those of you who had arms, with a very few exceptions, have left them at home, and those who had Government horses have failed to report them here. Now let me say to you once and all, those of you who have retained your arms, as soon as you get home take them to the nearest military post and deliver them up, or burn them, or get rid of them in some manner, for as sure as there is a God in heaven if they are found in your houses, just so sure will your houses be burned to the ground, and I hope to God every one of you who keep good arms or property of any kind in your homes will be hanged, and you will too.

The surrender negotiations and events at Chalk Bluff and Jacksonport are relatively unknown outside the region. (jsp)

Be good citizens, and then those of you have been good, honest, and brave soldiers have nothing to fear, but I warn those of you who have been nothing but sneaking cowardly jay-hawkers, cut-throats, and thieves, that a just retribution awaits you and I hope to God that the Federal authorities will hang you wherever and whenever they find you, and they'll do it, sure.

After finishing, Thompson left the ship, made his way through the crowd to the hotel where had been staying, and paid his bill with his horse saddle, having no money. He then returned to the steamship.

Davis wrote that "the first reaction to the end of the long hard years was a stunned relief." He also noted the

Confederate conditions: "No transportation except 300 or 400 dugout canoes, No public animals, Less than 500 arms, No food." Over the next few days Union troops issued 28,000 rations of sugar, salt, coffee, vinegar, and hardtack.

One of the Union officers, Dr. Charles Brackett, wrote in his journal about using the home of Mary Tom Caldwell: "She gave up the house with a tolerable good graces. She said to me, 'She wished to kill every officer in our Army and Old Abe especially.'"

*   *   *

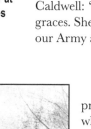

Jacksonport witnessed the formation of troops at the start of the war, their surrender at its end, and in the decades after, many reunions of veterans—including this gathering of the Jackson Guards in 1914. (jsp)

Jacksonport State Park in Arkansas preserves the old town site and the waterfront where Thompson delivered his final address. It was the site of postwar reunions, and meetings of the United Daughters of the Confederacy. Yet commerce slowly declined. In 1892 the county seat was moved to Newport, and by 1903 the town was largely abandoned. In 1962, the Jackson County Historical Society began to preserve historic buildings at the site, and it became a state park three years later.

A county-owned park commemorates the 1863 battle of Chalk Bluff, but there are no markers discussing the surrender negotiations there. A state historic marker stands at the site of Wittsburg to note the paroling of Confederates there. The town's commerce dwindled when a railroad bypassed the community in the 1880s. By 1900, its post office closed. Today the Wittsburg Natural Area preserves the area's natural history.

The Harrison County Historical Museum in Marshall, Texas, has exhibits on the town's Civil War history. A marker also notes the house that served as the capitol of the Missouri government in exile. Here Governor Thomas C. Reynolds and his staff directed the civil and military affairs of Confederate Missourians.

To visit sites associated with the surrenders in the Trans-Mississippi Theater:

Chalk Bluff Battlefield Park
County Road 368 St.
Francis, AR 72454

Jacksonport State Park
205 Avenue Street
Newport, AR 72075

Forts Randolph and Buhlow State Historic Site
135 Riverfront Street
Pineville, LA 71360

Harrison County Historical Museum
P.O. Box 1987
Marshall, TX

The bulk of Thompson's troops—more than 5,000—surrendered at Jacksonport, while another 2,000 laid down their arms at Wittsburg, to the south. (jsp)

The Nations Negotiate

CHAPTER FIFTEEN

JUNE-JULY 1865

The war in the Indian Territory (now Oklahoma) involved shifting alliances, guerilla warfare, and internal division.

In this theater, black, white, and Indians all fought together, sometimes in the same units. Union Indian regiments included different tribes by company, led by white or trusted Indian officers. Confederate Indian regiments were organized by tribe, led by native leaders. All told, the Confederates raised 11 regiments and seven battalions of Indian cavalry, and more served in the ranks of white units.

The Cherokee were divided, with many reluctant to break their treaties with the United States. Chief John Ross pushed neutrality in the conflict, but Chief Stand Watie would have none of it. Watie saw the conflict as one against a traditional enemy, the United States.

Watie, whose Cherokee name was De-ga-ta-ga, was the only Indian to achieve the rank of general in the Civil War. He was one of the Cherokee tribal leaders who consented to the removal from Georgia to Oklahoma. This split the tribe into two factions, and Watie took the helm of the minority group, which became the pro-Confederate faction when the war broke out; the majority group sided with the Union.

Watie organized a company, then a regiment: the First Cherokee Mounted Rifles. They saw action in engagements like Pea Ridge, as well as in numerous skirmishes in Arkansas and the Indian Territory.

As more Chickasaw, Choctaw, and Creek Indians

Today, the foundation remains of buildings at Fort Towson are preserved by the Oklahoma Historical Society and administered as a park.
(dr/b&g)

The only Native American on either side to achieve the rank of general, Stand Watie was a leader among the Cherokee long before the war erupted (left). General Grenville Dodge (right) initiated the effort to contact Watie about surrendering. (loc) (loc)

An important leader of the Cherokee, John Ross initially opposed siding with the Confederacy, then supported it. (loc)

expressed their desire to ally with the Confederacy, Chief John Ross altered his position, and the Cherokee Council voted for an alliance with the Confederacy in June 1861.

By 1865, Union forces held most of the settled parts of the Indian Territory, with Confederates controlling the southern part. On May 28, news arrived in the territory of Smith's surrender of the Department of Trans-Mississippi, which included the Indian Territory.

Stand Watie intended to keep fighting, though—but the tide was against him. Indian chiefs who disagreed convened the Grand Council on June 10 and passed resolutions calling for the Indian commanders to stop fighting. One of those who favored ending the fighting was Peter Pitchlynn, known as Hat-chico-tucknee, the principal Choctaw chief.

Knowing of the unrest among the tribes, Union Maj. Gen. Grenville Dodge appointed Lt. Col. Asa C. Matthews to negotiate a peace with the Indians. Matthews had commanded the 99th Illinois and fought most recently at Spanish Fort and Fort Blakeley near Mobile.

The Indian nations each negotiated separate treaties from other Confederate forces just as they had signed their own treaties with the Confederacy. On May 26, many of the tribes held a council affirming friendship with each other and pledging to make peace with the United States. Matthews learned of the conference too late to attend, but wrote to the chiefs that he approved of their actions and would follow up with them.

On June 19, Chief Peter Pitchlynn signed a treaty on behalf of the Choctaws and Caddos at Doaksville. All of the tribes looked forward to a larger conference at Fort Smith in September.

Once the largest town in Indian Territory and capital of the Choctaw Nation, Doaksville declined rapidly after the war. (ohs)

Three days later, on June 22, Watie and two aides spent the night at the Rose Hill Plantation owned by noted Choctaw Robert M. Jones, who had represented the Choctaws in the Confederate Congress. The next day, Watie and his aides rode to Doaksville where they met with Matthews and Lt. Col. William H. Vance at the Masonic Lodge, chartered from Arkansas—both Jones and Waite were Masons.

There, Watie surrendered the First Indian Cavalry Brigade, consisting of Cherokee, Creek, Seminole, and Osage troops. This was the last Confederate military force to formally surrender.

The treaty stipulated that the Indians "agree at once to return to their respective homes and there remain at peace with United States, and offer no indignities whatever against the whites or Indians of the various tribes who have been friendly to or engaged in the service of the United States during the war."

Article II stipulated that "the undersigned commissioners on part of the United States, that so long as the Indians aforesaid observe the provisions of article first of this agreement, they shall be protected by the United States authorities in their person and property, not only from encroachment on the part of the whites, but also from the Indians who have been engaged in the service of the United States."

Rather than a surrender, this was actually a treaty of peace, ending hostilities and returning the Cherokee to their former relationship with the United States government.

Each of the Indian nations ended the war the same way, with treaties affirming friendship and ending hostilities; they were not, in the true sense of the word,

Rose Hill (above) was owned by Choctaw Congressman Robert M. Jones. Stand Watie spent the night there before riding into Doaksville to surrender. Today nothing remains of the once-prosperous plantation, although a monument marks the site (below). (ohs) (ohs)

Monuments and markers commemorate the location of Watie's surrender at the Doaksville archeology site. (dr/b&g)

Brig. Gen. Douglass H. Cooper, Confederate Superintendent of Indian Affairs, carried out the terms of the Galveston surrender in the Indian Territory. (loc)

surrenders. The Indians were free to return to their homes and remain at peace with the United States. "There is a general desire among all the tribes to return to their homes and live in peace with each other and the United States," observed Brig. Gen. James Veatch, who was involved with the negotiations.

At Fort Washita on June 28, Brig. Gen. Douglass H. Cooper, the Confederate Superintendent of Indian Affairs, pledged to carry out the terms of the Galveston surrender for all of the white Confederate troops in the Indian Territory. This was a formality, showing that the terms of Kirby Smith's surrender were being carried out there.

On July 14, Governor Winchester Colbert of the Chickasaws surrendered to Matthews. This was the last tribe to surrender, and he was the last civil authority to surrender. The Creek and Seminole never formally surrendered.

The various tribal representatives hoped peace would come quickly, not only with the United States government, but among the tribes. "Peace and friendship shall forever exist between the tribes and bands. . . ." proclaimed one document. "The tomahawk shall be forever buried. The scalping knife shall be forever broken."

Doaksville was established as a trading post, and it served as the capital of the Choctaw Nation.

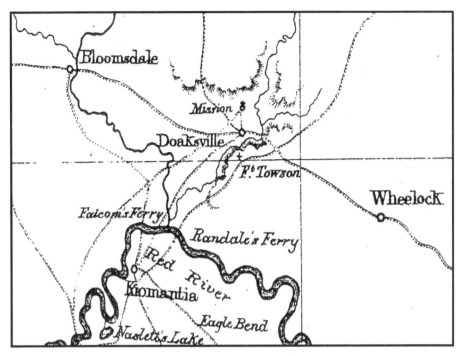

It was the largest town in the Indian Territory prior to the war. It included homes, stores, a jail, school, and two newspapers.

Nearby Fort Towson had been built to guard the southeastern border of the United States and protect the Cherokee in their new land. Abandoned in 1829, it was reoccupied the next year. From 1830-1836, it was along one of the main roads for settlers moving into Texas. In 1842, the log structures were rebuilt and, by 1846, it was a staging area for the Mexican War. Abandoned again in 1854, it became the offices of the Choctaw Indian agent until the war started. During the war, both Confederate troops and their Indian allies used the fort, and it served as a regional headquarters. After the fighting, many Confederate troops passed through the fort on their way home.

On September 14, representatives of the various tribes met with federal officials at Fort Smith, Arkansas, the main Union army post in the region. The delegates tried to heal the wounds and divisions of the war through negotiation, but were not entirely successful. In the resulting treaty, the Indians affirmed their loyalty to the United States, renounced all treaties with the Confederacy, and agreed to end slavery (admitting former slaves as tribal members). The Federal government wanted a single Indian government to work with, but

This historical map shows the locations of Fort Towson and Doaksville. The Red River, running along the southern edge, is the boundary with Texas. (ohs)

Built in 1831, Fort Towson was abandoned by 1855, although Confederates began using it in 1863 as their base of operations. In the years since the war, the ruins of the fort have attracted the interest of tourists. (ohs)

this goal was not realistic and failed to gain momentum. Tensions lingered between the pro-Union and pro-Confederate factions of the tribes.

Following the Civil War, Watie served as a member of the Southern Cherokee delegation during the negotiation of the Cherokee Reconstruction Treaty of 1866. He then abandoned public life and returned to his old home along Honey Creek. He died on September 9, 1871, and is buried in the Old Ridge Cemetery in Delaware County, Oklahoma.

Aside from the ruins at the site of Doaksville, there's also a cannon, covered by a small pavilion. (ohs)

After the war, Asa Matthews returned to Illinois and was a successful lawyer and United States Revenue Collector. He was also active in building a local railroad in Pike County. He died in 1908.

In 1870, the new St. Louis and San Francisco railroad bypassed Doaksville, signaling the end of this community—as had happened at Appomattox. The town was largely abandoned, and a new one sprung up near the railroad, taking the name of the old post: Fort Towson.

In the 1960s, the Oklahoma Historical Society acquired the historic town site. The Historical Society conducted archaeological work in the 1990s to document the ruins of the town, including the jail, several wells, a store, and hotel. The Doaksville Archaeological Site today includes stabilized ruins, walking trails, and signage that interprets the town's history.

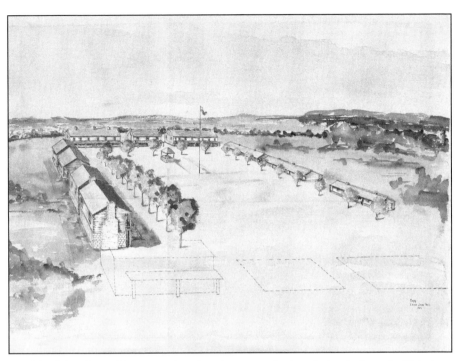

To visit points of interest related to the surrender in Indian Territory:

A sketch shows the historic layout of Fort Towson, including the footprints of missing buildings. (loc)

Fort Towson/Doaksville
HC 63, Box 1580
Fort Towson, OK 74735-9273
580.873.2634
http://www.okhistory.org/sites/ftdoaksville.php

Fort Smith National Historic Site
301 Parker Ave, Fort Smith, AR 72901
(479) 783-3961
www.nps.gov/fosm

Fort Gibson
907 N. Garrison
Fort Gibson, OK 74434
918.478.4088
fortgibson@okhistory.org

Fort Washita
3348 State Rd. 199
Star Route 213
Durant, OK 74701-9443
580.924.6502
ftwashita@okhistory.org

The Surrender in Memory

CHAPTER SIXTEEN

APRIL 1865-PRESENT

When Lee surrendered to Grant on April 9, he only surrendered the Army of Northern Virginia. The stature of Lee was so great that his downfall signaled the virtual end of the Confederacy's military effort.

Although each Confederate army had to surrender individually, and would by June, inevitably whenever Union troops encountered Confederate units after Appomattox, they approached them with the mindset that the war was over, if not in fact, in reality. When Union troops met small garrisons or isolated Confederate units after early April, they approached them with the expectation that they would surrender, and many Confederate troops in fact agreed in that assumption. Of course, some still held out hope of resistance, including the large forces of Taylor and Smith, as well as isolated garrisons scattered across the Deep South. However, the Union and Confederates alike saw Appomattox as the symbolic end of the war.

Ironically, the best-known surrender was not only the smallest, it was the least representative of the war's ending. Appomattox did set the reconciliatory tone for lenient terms, but the presence of the war's two top commanders—and its two primary armies—has overshadowed the other events.

Analyzing the surrenders reveals that in only one case was there a final battle where the two armies were in physical contact, and in which arrangements were made in only one meeting: Appomattox.

The other surrenders share similarities with each

Stacked muskets in Petersburg after the collapse of the Confederate line and the fall of the city (loc)

"The End of the Rebellion in the United States" was sequel to Christopher Kimmel's grand image "The Outbreak of the Rebellion in the United States" issued the year before. According to the Library of Congress, "[T]he artist depicts in symbolic terms the downfall of the Confederacy. Columbia, crowned with stars, and Liberty, wearing a Phrygian cap and holding an American flag, stand on a pedestal in the center. On the pedestal are carved the likenesses of George Washington and Abraham Lincoln. In front of the pedestal, Justice, armed with sword and scales, leads a charge of Union troops toward the right. Immediately behind Justice stands President Andrew Johnson, and behind him Union generals Butler, Grant, and Sherman are visible. A black soldier stands in the foreground and a freed slave kneels before Liberty's pedestal. An eagle bearing thunderbolts flies overhead, also toward the right, where the vanquished Confederates are gathered. Jefferson Davis (holding a sack of money), Robert E. Lee (offering his sword in surrender), and John Wilkes Booth (with a pistol and knife) are prominent among them. In the distance are a leaning palmetto tree with a dead serpent hanging limp from it and (beyond) Fort Sumter flying an American flag." (loc)

other: armies widely separated; multiple meetings in different locations; delays and prolonged waiting; mass desertion; and lawlessness. Yet each was unique as well.

West of the Mississippi, it was obvious to the participants that the war was over as soon as they saw the former soldiers from all of the more eastern armies passing through to return to their homes. Their decision to break camp and return to their homes is, while technically desertion, more logically a resignation of their duties to the Confederacy, replacing it with their higher duty to family and self.

The largest surrender was at the Bennett Place. Only one took place onboard a ship, in Galveston harbor. One was forced by subordinates, Galveston, and one was forced by the troops themselves, Chalk Bluff. And only one site preserves the original home, on the same location, with the original furniture, the Magee farm. Only one has a monument to reunification, the Bennett Place.

It was an uneasy transition to peace—the Union government and military had focused its effort on the war, and reconstruction efforts were still experimental and controversial. It was equally chaotic for soldiers who were suddenly civilians, for civilians who were suddenly occupied, and for former slaves who had to make their way in society. The changes were unprecedented, and the one thing that everyone faced that summer was uncertainty.

Throughout the rest of the summer, small bands continued to surrender, seeking paroles. Others fled. On July 12, Maj. Gen. Jo Shelby led a group of 500 riders across the Rio Grande at Eagle Pass, Texas. With the war behind them, they hoped for a new future in Mexico. It is estimated that as many as 10,000 fled the former Confederacy for Mexico, England, Canada, Brazil, and even Japan.

On November 6, 1865, the crew of the C.S.S. *Shenandoah* steered the ship into Liverpool, lowered the flag, and disbanded. The last Confederate military force was gone.

Fewer than half of all Confederate soldiers in 1865 surrendered as part of the famous armies like the Army of Northern Virginia or the Army of Tennessee. Fewer still received paroles; the vast majority of Confederate soldiers—no matter where they were—simply went home.

On August 20, 1866, President Andrew Johnson declared the War officially over. By then the country had entered the bewildering and insecure world of Reconstruction.

*   *   *

The enduring legacy of Appomattox overshadowed the other surrenders and has influenced understandings of the end of the conflict up to our own time. Appomattox was first, giving it the chance to influence all subsequent events. It also involved the two most famous commanders, and the two principal armies, of each side.

Moreover, Appomattox unfolded with a neat, seamless process in which the fighting ended and was largely accepted by the vanquished, and the victors generally showed compassion. Yet none of the other surrenders followed that precedent; all the rest were marked with confusion, bitterness, tension, delay, and ambiguity. The Appomattox story satisfies the need for a neat, comforting closure to the war.

Perhaps it was too easy for those present in 1865 to see Appomattox as the end of the struggle. A century earlier and 150 miles to the east, the surrender of the British at Yorktown effectively ended the Revolutionary War, though it took nearly two more years of negotiation to produce a final treaty.

Yet there was no final treaty to be had in 1865. The Union government did not recognize the Confederacy as a separate nation. The Southern soldiers just went home, and Union troops occupied the region. There were no boundary issues to settle, no trade agreements to hammer out, no international issues to wrangle with, and certainly no Confederate government to treat with by May of 1865.

The 1783 Treaty of Paris was acceptable to both sides, yet left them each dissatisfied. Lingering issues led to a second conflict between Britain and the United States in 1812. Yet the resolution reached at Appomattox seemed final. The war was over, and a new order was in place. There were social tensions and unresolved internal issues about race, civil rights, and government, yet the questions of military resistance and Southern independence were ended for good. Perhaps this is why the Appomattox appeal has been so strong.

For Southern civilians, the transition to peacetime was slow and gradual, yet for the soldiers of both armies, it was uncomfortably rapid. Overnight, Confederate soldiers became civilians, and Union troops became occupies and peacekeepers. Neither had time to fully adjust to their new realities, and Reconstruction would be a long, rocky road ahead of them.

A sketch of the village of Appomattox Court House (loc)

*   *   *

Although it was a famous and important place, people rarely visited small and isolated Appomattox Court House. The town also had some bad luck after the war. The railroad station was a few miles away, and more

traffic passed through there than on the stagecoach road. Eventually, Appomattox Station eclipsed the village. Aiding in its decline was an 1893 fire that destroyed the courthouse. Citizens voted to build a new courthouse at Appomattox Station.

Soon the village of Appomattox Court House was abandoned except for a few families. At the railroad station, the modern town of Appomattox grew, especially with the new courthouse to attract businesses and residents.

Wilmer McLean did not build the house that was used for the surrender meeting. He and his family had lived near Manassas, the site of the first major battle of the war. The movement of armies there hurt his business as a merchant, though, so he looked to relocate. In 1863, about half way through the war, he and his family moved to Appomattox. It is ironic that the armies would meet again in his parlor.

The surrender did not bring him fame and fortune, though. After the war he was heavily in debt and had to move his family back to Northern Virginia.

In the 1890s, a group of investors bought the McLean house, intending to move it to Washington, D.C., as a Civil War museum. The house was disassembled brick by brick, but then the group ran out of money, and the materials sat in place. Over time, weather and souvenir hunters took their toll on the bricks and lumber.

Despite good intentions, the McLean House was disassembled and then abandoned, left to the elements and souvenir hunters. In the 1950s, the Park Service rebuilt the home, using as many original bricks as possible. (achnhp)

Historic Appomattox: "Where the Nation Reunited" (cm)

Despite the disassembly of the house, the village of Appomattox still drew attention from veterans for decades. One plan called for a retirement village there for both Union and Confederate veterans. However, the only monuments placed at the site were by the state of North Carolina, marking the position of troops in the last battle, erected in 1905. Congress approved a Reunification Monument for the site, but funding never materialized and it was never built.

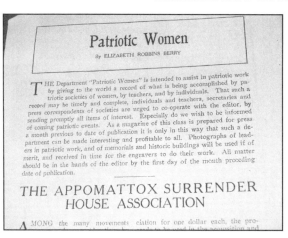

The Appomattox Surrender House Association was one of many failed efforts to commemorate the site before the National Park Service became involved. (bd)

Route 24 ran through the old village, passing yards from the McLean house steps, until rerouted in 1940. The same year, Congress created a National Park at the site. The work of restoring the buildings began, though it was interrupted by World War II. Two of the most ambitious projects were reconstructing the courthouse and McLean house—using as many original bricks as could be found. The Park Service restoration took place at a time when reconstruction of historic sites was in vogue. About half the structures in the village are rebuilt.

The modern town of Appomattox has adopted "Where our nation reunited" as its tourism slogan. It speaks to the reassuring notion of a peaceful resolution, and final closure. Yet Appomattox, as smoothly as it went, still had its rocky moments, and it was not the end of the

war. Reunification would be a long time in coming, and didn't happen in any one place.

The preservation of Appomattox received national attention, but in Durham, North Carolina, local citizens made the effort to preserve and mark the events that took place at the Bennett farm. The Bennetts continued to reside at the home until 1889. In 1921, after sitting abandoned for years, the house caught fire.

At the same time, local leaders formed the Bennett Place Memorial Commission to preserve the site. In 1923, they erected a granite monument on the site with two columns representing the North and South and the word "Unity" inscribed across the top. No such memorial stands at Appomattox, the better-known site.

That same year, the commission conveyed the site to the state of North Carolina. In 1959, the state began restoring the surviving buildings, and the home was reconstructed using material from a nearby period home. The state still operates Bennett Place as a state historic site.

The only surrender that maintained a living legacy was in Citronelle, where the Surrender Oak stood until 1906, long after Taylor and Canby departed. The Citronelle Depot Museum interprets the town's history, including the meeting on April 4, 1865. They also

Restoration of the Bennett Place site began in earnest in 1921 after the original farmhouse burned. Only the chimney remained (bottom). A Unity monument was soon erected, buildings were eventually rebuilt, and the site was restored (above). (cm)(cm)

Large-scale commemoration of the Civil War's 150th anniversary kicked off with an event at Manassas National Battlefield Park in 2011. (bd)

sponsor the annual Surrender Oak Festival, focused on local history.

The Magee farm, the only original surrender house in its original location, faces an uncertain future. Although past owners kept the original furniture intact, the passionate work by Dr. Ben George of Mobile to run the site as a museum failed due to low visitation—which speaks to the long shadow of Appomattox as the perceived end of the war.

Long-neglected in traditional Civil War studies, the surrender process of the Trans-Mississippi has almost no tangible remnants today. Several markers in Marshall, Texas, recall the town's importance to the Confederacy, but none note the surrender. Shreveport, the site of the army's camps and the Department headquarters, has no markers testifying to these events.

An enduring legacy of the war's end has been the site of the last cabinet meeting. Historic markers in Danville, Virginia; Charlotte, North Carolina; Fort Mill, and Abbeville, South Carolina; and Washington, Georgia, all proclaim the event. Each community, relatively untouched by the war until its final weeks, desired to lay claim to its final ending. If details matter, the entire group's last meeting took place in Charlotte on

April 26 in the upstairs west room at the Phifer house on North Tryon Street.

"Lasts" tend to capture the imagination, much as "firsts" do. A marker stands near Waynesville, North Carolina, commemorating the "Last Shot" of the war east of the Mississippi River. Here on May 6, Lt. Robert Conley led a small group from Thomas' Legion against Union troopers from the 2nd North Carolina Mounted Infantry—a clash between Union and Confederate North Carolinians. The last man killed east of the Mississippi River was Union soldier James Arwood, and afterwards, Conley often stated, "I still have James Arwood's gun as a relic."

The ending of the war was as complicated, and events were as widespread, as they were at the war's beginning, yet the war's end has received far less attention from historians. The closing of the conflict, just like its start, was a transitional period. By 1865, Reconstruction was already well underway in some places, and the new realities of postwar life were setting in more deeply everywhere as the weeks passed by that spring. The ending of the war reveals a great deal about how Reconstruction would unfold, and how the conflict would—and would not—be remembered and commemorated.

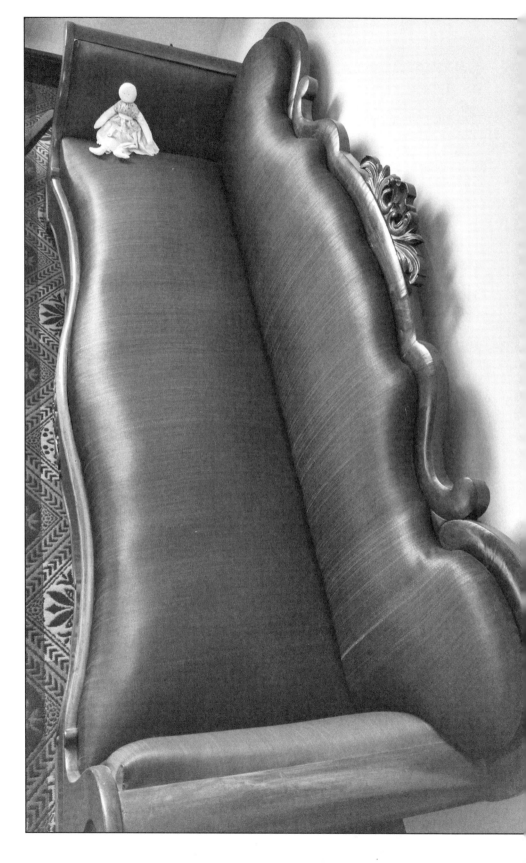

The Surrenders at a Glance

APPENDIX A

Appomattox, Virginia—April 9, 1865	28,231
Bennett Place, North Carolina—April 26, 1865	89,270
Citronelle, Alabama—May 4, 1865	42,293
Chalk Bluff, Arkansas—May 11, 1865	7,806
Galveston, Texas—June 2, 1865	58,650
TOTAL:	**226,250**

The numbers here represent, as best as can be determined, the final numbers at the time of surrender.

The dates and locations of Citronelle and Galveston appear here instead of the Magee farm and New Orleans because they are the final surrender meeting locations, whereas the earlier locations were only preliminary meetings.

The sofa in the McLean house
is one of the few original
pieces in the parlor. (dd)

The USCTs in the Appomattox Campaign

APPENDIX B

BY CHRISTOPHER BINGHAM

During the winter of 1864-65, the Federal armies of Lt. Gen. Ulysses S. Grant were reorganized. All of the United States Colored Troops in the Richmond-Petersburg area were consolidated into the new XXV Corps. This force was commanded by Maj. Gen. Godfrey Weitzel and served as part of the Army of the James.

The seven units that were ultimately involved in the Appomattox campaign included the 8th, 29th, 31st, 41st, 45th, 116th, and 127th United States Colored Troops. The 8th USCT, organized in Philadelphia during 1863, had fought at the battle of Olustee, Florida. The 29th and 31st, formed in early 1864 in Illinois and New York, had suffered heavy casualties at the battle of the Crater. The 116th USCT was raised in Kentucky, while the remaining three units were organized in Philadelphia. These regiments, all raised in the summer and fall of 1864, had largely avoided the worst of combat during their time in the siege lines outside of Petersburg and Richmond.

Although these seven units—numbering close to 5,000 men—had different origins and combat experience, their composition was similar. As per nearly all USCT regiments, white officers commanded the troops. The men themselves largely reflected black society in America in the mid-nineteenth century. A significant minority of the soldiers were Northern-born free men, particularly from northeastern cities; many others were free blacks from slave states. A small percentage were foreign born, particularly from Canada and the Caribbean. However, the majority of the rank and file was made up of those who had escaped bondage in the Confederacy or attained their freedom in the pro-Union border states.

On the night of March 27, 1865, as Grant began his final offensive against the Army of Northern Virginia and the city of Petersburg, the 2nd Division of the XXV Corps, commanded by Brig. Gen. William Birney, crossed the James River and participated in the movement. The black troops were joined by two white divisions of the XXIV Corps. Although Birney's soldiers avoided any serious fighting, they were among some of the first Federal troops to march into Petersburg on the morning of April 3.

The African American Civil War Memorial in Washington, D.C., lists the name of every African-American soldier and sailor who fought in the war.
(nps)

United States Colored Troops played ever increasing roles in the final months of the war, fighting in every theater. (nps)

As Lee's army retreated westward and Grant's followed, the USCTs were utilized to secure the South Side Railroad. Not until April 7, as the armies converged on Farmville, would Birney's soldiers get their chance to actively participate in the vital campaign. The two brigades, under Cols. Ulysses Doubleday (8th, 41st, 45th, and 127th) and William Woodward (29th, 31st, and 116th), were now temporarily attached to the white troops of the XXIV Corps.

As Lee's troops marched west on April 8, the USCTs and the remainder of the Army of the James force-marched, paralleling the South Side Railroad in an attempt to cut off the Confederate retreat at Appomattox Station. After marching nearly 30 miles in less than 20 hours, the white and black troops reached the vicinity of the station around 1:30 a.m. During this Herculean feat, there was little or no straggling among the troops. "[I]n an experience of more than three years I never witnessed greater powers of endurance," one Federal surgeon observed.

Meanwhile, early on the morning of April 9, Confederate infantry and cavalry attacked the Union cavalry roadblock just west of the village of Appomattox Court House. This final attempt to escape Grant's

APPENDIX B: The USCTs in the Appomattox Campaign   151

clutches was initially successful until the Army of the James arrived on the field. Advancing to the left of the developing battle line, Doubleday's Brigade—minus the 127th USCT, left to guard the supply wagons—quickly drove back a force of Confederate cavalry. Meanwhile, Woodward's Brigade moved forward amidst the white troops of the XXIV Corps and advanced toward the Confederate infantry astride the Richmond-Lynchburg Stage Road.

The arrival of Federal infantry forced Lee to order his troops to fall back. Flags of truce soon went out, and the Confederate commander surrendered his army that afternoon.

The battle of Appomattox Court House, though of relatively short duration and producing fewer than 700 casualties, proved to be one of most decisive engagements of the Civil War. The USCTs, suffering barely a half-dozen casualties, had played a key role in blocking the Confederate escape route. The resulting surrender of the Army of Northern Virginia quickly proved the beginning of the end of the war, assuring the restoration of the Union and the abolition of slavery.

One USCT, speaking of the experience years later, recalled: "I was with General Grant when Lee surrendered at Appomattox. . . . That was freedom."

CHRISTOPHER BINGHAM
is a park ranger at Appomattox Court House National Historical Park. He has previously worked at Pamplin Park and Petersburg National Battlefield.

The Long Road Home from Appomattox

APPENDIX C

BY ERNIE K. PRICE

According to the terms agreed to in the McLean house, the Confederates were to be paroled in exchange for surrendering their military equipment. This generous offer meant they would not go to prison and would be allowed to utilize, where available, federally controlled transportation and warehouses.

Despite this generosity, the majority of these men would walk most of the way home.

Two-thirds of Lee's army was infantry, and their designated day to lay down arms was April 12. By late afternoon, many were already receiving their parole passes and starting their journeys home. The fact that men left that afternoon suggests an eagerness to be away from the final resting place of the Army of Northern Virginia. It may have been too tempting to start for home, rather than sleep on it and get a good start in the morning. More practically, the prospects of better food and a more comfortable night's sleep even a few miles down the road lured men to leave immediately.

There were soldiers from Virginia's Shenandoah Valley and from Tennessee—and there were even those who had reasons to travel north—that led some to take non-southerly routes out of Appomattox. A noticeable fraction of Deep Southerners actually backtracked east, over the route of the last campaign, headed toward the navigable portions of the James River below Richmond. These men boarded ships for the Chesapeake and the Atlantic coast southward.

The bulk of the men, though, understood that the closest railhead leading south was in Danville, Virginia, and thousands on April 12 and 13 headed that way. On April 16, Danville's population swelled while rumors spread about when the next train would arrive. The former soldiers no doubt envisioned themselves riding the rails to Greensboro and perhaps even all the way to Charlotte, taking them that much closer to home. When the train arrived the next day, men occupied every possible inch: inside, outside, and on top of the cars. Others looked on and decided against becoming a sardine and elected to continue walking.

Confederates traveled by foot and by rail, traveling from Appomattox to as far away as Texas. (dd)

Many of the riders would be disappointed when 10

Once hostilities ended, soldiers from both armies mingled freely. Federals traded for souvenirs; Confederates traded for provisions that would help see them through the long journey home. (nps)

miles north of Greensboro the train stopped at a broken bridge. Being relegated to walking status again was eased a bit by no longer being a sardine, and the realization that, given the condition of the cars and tracks, the train didn't travel much faster anyway.

As for rates of travel, motivated soldiers going south reached the North Carolina line five days after leaving Appomattox. Georgians, on average, crossed the Savannah River the first week of May. A group of Texans sailed into Galveston on June 2—ironically, the day that the Trans-Mississippi Department was surrendered in that same city.

There were common challenges for the travelers. The first was deciding whether to maintain their regimental organization or go in smaller groups. Within two days of leaving Appomattox, they realized that smaller groups of two to six men were more effective. They quickly learned that, when 50 to 100 men showed up at a farm seeking food and shelter, even the most patriotic Southern citizens could offer little. Small groups, on the other hand, were often welcomed, fed something, and offered some form of shelter in either a barn, on a porch, or, on special occasions, even a bed. The travelers were routinely told that there was a man or boy from that household in the war and, wherever he was, the homeowner hoped that someone was taking care of him that night.

Other challenges typically included crossing large rivers, waiting for ferries or ships. Certain soldiers who passed through the Raleigh corridor had to contend with a particularly barren landscape already heavily picked over by Sherman's army. All soldiers were affected by the news of Lincoln's assassination, fueling paranoia about encountering Federal troops at stations and "occupied" towns along the way.

Some soldiers in the 5th Florida Infantry faced a particularly ugly challenge. According to one of their members, twice along their route home—once at City Point, Virginia, and again in Savannah, Georgia—they encountered United States Colored Troops serving as guards. In both cases, the encounters resulted in disagreements and the murder of one of the blacks at each location, with the travelers escaping.

Though most soldiers came to terms with Lee's surrender and were satisfied with his message to them in his General Order Number 9—that they had done their duty and it was time to go home—there were some who felt they could not surrender. In mid-April, soldiers from the Greensboro, North Carolina, area were faced with the reality that the Confederate Army of Tennessee was in the vicinity of their home, and a collision with Sherman's army was possible. The war was not over: their homes were still vulnerable.

Common to all who made it home was the moment when they felt they were near the place they had dreamed of so many times. Invariably, after dozens or hundreds of miles, no matter how much or how little assistance was gained from trains, ships, or wagons, the veteran found himself on foot as he neared home. Typically he spotted something that was unique to his memory of home: an intersection, a bridge, a store, a church, or even a certain view of the mountains. He typically met someone he knew before he reunited with his family: a neighbor, a preacher, a former member of his regiment already home, or a distant relative. He got updates about his family and the neighborhood until the final fork in the road. This was the moment when he parted with his travel companion(s), his comrades, his brothers in arms. He walked out of soldierhood and into his future—and this walk he made alone.

Waiting for many was a familiar fence or yard, the muscle memory of that step onto the front porch, a dog, and of course the moment of reintroduction to a sister, father, and the taste of mother's best meal.

Though the place was the same, the people were forever changed, perhaps the soldier most of all. The future was nothing anyone could know or have imagined four years earlier.

ERNIE PRICE *is the chief of interpretation at Appomattox Court House National Historical Park. A native of the area, he has been researching the journey home of Confederate soldiers for many years.*

The Last Act:
The Surrender of the C.S.S. Shenandoah

APPENDIX D
BY CHRISTOPHER L. KOLAKOWSKI

Day after day, a lonely light shone at the southern end of St. George's Channel, running between Britain and Ireland. For many a northbound mariner, this light meant the nearness of destination, especially one of the ports on either side of the Irish Sea.

On a cold and foggy night in November 1865, a three-masted ship passed the light and hove to near another light, this one at the Mersey Bar, where the Mersey River meets the open sea. She signaled for a pilot to take her in to Liverpool. As the pilot clambered aboard, he asked the name of the ship. Her captain answered with the name C.S.S. *Shenandoah*. "I was reading a few days ago of your being in the Arctic Ocean," exclaimed the surprised pilot.

The last Confederate force on the planet had reached port.

Shenandoah took a long and adventurous road to this moment. Launched in 1863 as the *Sea King*, the Confederate government purchased her for conversion into an armed merchant cruiser. To maintain Britain's neutrality, the *Sea King* was purchased by a front and put to sea ostensibly headed on a voyage to India. In Madeira, she met another ship, the *Laurel*, carrying weapons, implements of war, and Confederate officers. On October 19, 1864, the *Sea King* became C.S.S. *Shenandoah*.

The ship's captain, Commander James I. Waddell of North Carolina, received orders to go to the Pacific and hunt Union whalers off Australia, New Zealand, Russia, and in the Bering Sea. After that, his orders offered this cryptic guidance: "Your ship will probably be in want of repairs, and it may be necessary for you to decide what disposition could be advantageously made of her." With that in mind, Waddell set off on his mission.

Over the next months *Shenandoah* passed through the South Atlantic, around Cape Horn, and roamed the Indian Ocean and the waters around Australia. She captured or burned nine ships before docking at Melbourne, Australia, on January 25, 1865, for repairs and replenishment, leaving February 19.

In early April, she took several prizes in the Caroline

This historical cartoon was titled "The old rip of the SHENANDOAH." In it, Shenandoah Captain Waddell (as Rip Van Winkle) says, "Law! Mr. Pilot, you don't say so! The war in America over these eight months? Dear! dear! Who'd ever a' thought it!" (loc)

Before she went round the world, the C.S.S. *Shenandoah* **already had international roots. British-designed, Scottish-built, and India-bound, she was originally slated for use as a commercial transport in the East India tea trade.** (cphcw)

Islands and proceeded into the northern latitudes. After weeks of futile searching in the Sea of Okhotsk, Shenandoah arrived in the Bering Sea and found rich pickings among the New England whaling fleet. In six days from June 22 to June 28, she captured 23 Union ships, an average of nearly 4 per day. This success occurred with little fanfare or gunfire; reported Waddell, "The last gun in defense of the South was fired on the 22d of June, Arctic Ocean."

During this time, Waddell and his crew were not oblivious to developments on land. Newspapers reached them via the ships they encountered, giving news of the surrender of Robert E. Lee's Army of Northern Virginia and Jefferson Davis' proclamation to continue fighting.

Waddell decided to attack San Francisco, but on August 2 encountered a British ship that provided definite news of Davis's capture, Gen. Edmund Kirby Smith's surrender, and the collapse of the Confederacy. "Having received by the bark *Barracouta* the sad intelligence of the overthrow of the Confederate government," recorded the ship's log, "all attempts to destroy the shipping or property of the United States will cease from this date." *Shenandoah's* executive officer, Lieutenant William Whittle of Norfolk, Virginia, supervised the disarming of the ship.

Shenandoah was now the last sovereign Confederate territory on Earth. Captain Waddell and his crew faced a choice. "I had . . . a responsibility of the highest nature resting upon me in deciding the course we should pursue," he recalled, "which involved not only our personal honor, but the honor of the flag entrusted to us which had walked the waters fearlessly and in triumph."

Correctly fearing he and his men would be treated as pirates by U.S. authorities, Waddell decided to go to Liverpool, where he hoped to get a favorable reception. Over the next three months *Shenandoah* made her way around South America and northward toward the St. George's Channel—a distance of 17,000 miles. It was not an easy voyage, and the knowledge of Confederate defeat dampened the crew's spirits further. *Shenandoah* came within sight of the USS *Saranac* on October 25, but did not attract attention from the Union ship. A few days from Liverpool, the crew buried two men who succumbed to disease—the *Shenandoah's* only losses in a year of service on some of the Earth's toughest waters.

Shenandoah arrived at the Mersey Bar shortly before midnight on November 5. The next morning, she entered Liverpool Harbor and anchored near the frigate H.M.S. *Donegal*, which happened to be in port that day. "The fog shut out the town from our view," recalled a crewman, "and we were not sorry for it, for we did not care to have [a] gaping crowd on shore witness the humiliation that was soon to befall our ship."

The *Donegal's* captain, James A. Paynter, boarded *Shenandoah* "to ascertain the name of the vessel and gave me official intelligence of the termination of the American war," recalled Waddell. "He was polite." Waddell handed over a letter addressed to Lord Russell, British Foreign Secretary, in which he gave up *Shenandoah* to Her Majesty's Government. "I do not consider that I have a right to destroy her or any further right to command her," he declared.

At 10 a.m., November 6, 1865, James Waddell ordered the Confederate flag lowered. After 58,000 miles, 38 ships captured, and the only circumnavigation of the globe by the Confederate ship, C.S.S. *Shenandoah's* career was over. She, along with the Confederacy she served, now passed into history.

North Carolinian James I. Waddell had served twenty-two years in the U.S. Navy, including a stint as an instructor at the Naval Academy, before resigning his commission at the outset of the war. (don)

John Grimball served as a lieutenant on the *Shenandoah*. (loc)

For two days the officers and men stayed on board *Shenandoah* while the British government decided what to do. On the evening of November 8, the answer came. According to the Liverpool *Mercury*:

About 6 o'clock . . . a telegram was received from the Government by Captain Paynter . . . that the whole of the officers and crew, who were not British subjects were to be immediately paroled. Captain Paynter immediately proceeded to the Rock Ferry slip, and applied for a steamboat. The Rock Ferry steamer Bee was placed at his disposal by Mr. Thwaites, in which he immediately proceeded alongside the Shenandoah. Captain Paynter went on board and communicated to the officers the object of his visit. The crew were mustered on the quarterdeck by the officers of the ship, the roll book was brought out, and the names of the men called out as they occurred. As each man answered to his name he was asked what countryman he was. In not one instance did any of them acknowledge to be British citizens. Many nations were represented among them, but the majority claimed to be natives of the Southern States of America or "Southern citizens". Several of those however, who purported to be Americans, had an unmistakably Scotch accent, and seemed more likely to have hailed from the banks of the Clyde than the Mississippi. Captain Paynter informed the men that by order of the Government they were all paroled, and might proceed at once to shore. This intelligence was received by the men with every demonstration of joy, and they seemed to be delighted at the prospect of leaving the craft in which they had hoped to be able to assist the Southern Confederacy. They commenced to pack up their bedding and other articles as fast as possible, and conveyed on board the Bee, which was to take them to the landing stage. Before leaving the vessel, however, they gave three lusty cheers, for Captain Waddell, their late commander. Captain Waddell, in feeling terms, acknowledged the compliment, and said that he hoped the men would always behave themselves, as brave sailors ought to do. The men then went aboard the Bee, and were conveyed to the landing stage. This separated the Shenandoah and her crew.

C.S.S. *Shenandoah* was no more.

The United States took possession of *Shenandoah* and sailed her to America. In 1866, the Sultan of Zanzibar bought her and named her *El Majidi*. She sank in a storm off Zanzibar in 1872.

The C.S.S. *Shenandoah* based
on a wartime sketch (loc)

Waddell and most of his officers remained abroad for some years, eventually returning to the United States under various amnesties. The *Shenandoah's* foreign-born crew went home or signed onto other ships.

H.M.S. *Donegal* outlasted all the actors in this final drama, becoming the Royal Navy's torpedo school under the name H.M.S. *Vernon* until being broken up in 1923.

CHRISTOPHER L. KOLAKOWSKI, *a historian with Emerging Civil War, serves as director of the General Douglas MacArthur Memorial in Norfolk, Virginia. He is the author of several books on the Civil War and World War Two, and has particular expertise in Civil War naval affairs.*

BELLE GROVE
PLANTATION
1797
A National Trust Historic Site
← ENTRANCE

The Lost Generation

APPENDIX E

BY SHANNON MOECK

When President Abraham Lincoln called for 75,000 troops after the firing on Ft. Sumter, Confederate President Jefferson Davis responded two days later with a call for 32,000 troops. Men rushed to enlist. Most regiments comprised of men from the same families and neighbors of the same region.

This type of grouping of men would be dire for the continuance of certain regions and family legacies: companies raised from the same communities caused these areas to lose an entire generation of men. The Pelican Rifles, a company in the 2nd Louisiana Volunteers, is an extreme example of this. Of the 151 men who served in the unit, 119 died in the war. Of the 32 who survived, 31 were wounded. Imagine the impact on areas devastated by such loss.

"They die, these brave and noble boys, but they live," proclaimed an editorial in the November 5, 1864, issue of *Harper's Weekly*. "They live in our purer purpose, in our firmer resolution in the surer justice of the nation. Against compromise, against concession, against surrender, this precious blood cries from the ground."

The words were written in an effort to let the public know their brave young men were dying for something worthwhile. Even though they were written for a Northern audience, the South felt just as sure that their cause was worth the sacrifice that war inflicted.

In total, more than 620,000 deaths—perhaps as many as 750,000—and more than one million total casualties occurred during the Civil War, for both the North and South. These numbers are staggering—yet numbers turn individual lives into statistics. However, each number reflects a life. Each person had a personal story, a life that included family, friends, careers, hobbies and passions.

The majority of these deaths came from one generation of Americans born between 1835-1845. This "Lost Generation" included men who were in their twenties and thirties while fighting in the Civil War. Two men who serve as examples of this Lost Generation were Stephen Dodson Ramseur and Charles Russell Lowell, Jr. Their stories individualize two of the "numbers." They both fought valiantly during their service in the Civil War until their fates were determined at the battle of Cedar Creek, Virginia, in October 1864.

An obelisk stands near the entrance to Belle Grove plantation on the Cedar Creek battlefield to commemorate Stephen Ramseur's mortal wounding during the battle.
(cm)

Stephen Dodson Ramseur was born on May 31,

Charles Rusell Lowell, Jr.
(left) and his wife, Josephine
"Effie" Shaw (right) (loc)(w/js)

1837, in Lincolnton, North Carolina. Charles Russell Lowell, Jr., was born on January 2, 1835, in Boston, Massachusetts. Both men led parallel yet different lives. Ramseur believed deeply in the Christian faith, while Lowell was raised in the Transcendentalist philosophy. Education was important to both young men—Ramseur a graduate of West Point and Lowell of Harvard University. At the brink of war, both men believed strongly in their respective nation's missions, and both enlisted for the cause they believe just.

Ramseur and Lowell had wartime weddings. While recuperating after his first wounding at Malvern Hill, Ramseur fell in love with his cousin Ellen Richmond. They were married on October 28, 1863. Lowell, meanwhile, set his eyes on the younger sister of his friend Robert Gould Shaw, Josephine, known affectionately as "Effie." In a sequence of events that paralleled Ramseur's romance, there was an awakening, a whirlwind courtship, and an engagement. Josephine Shaw and Charles Russell Lowell were married on October 31, 1863—three days after the Ramseurs.

Both men met their fate on October 19, 1864, during the battle of Cedar Creek when they were both mortally wounded during a Federal counterattack. They each died two weeks short of their first wedding anniversaries. Ramseur died just days after his daughter, Mary, was born;

The marker that commemorates Lowell's mortal wounding in battle sits in the front yard of an inn in Middletown—nowhere near the location of his actual wounding, which is today the south parking lot of Lord Fairfax Community College. (sm)

Lowell died weeks before his daughter, Carlotta, was born. Mary and Carlotta are two examples of the many children who would never know their fathers.

Ramseur had shown such promise in life. His affection for his family, his honor both at school and in battle, as well as his deep devotion to his faith, made this man. "He was a man who lived as he thought right and died as a consequence," said historian George Kundahl. "In sum, Ramseur's precepts and beliefs epitomize many of those

Stephen Dodson Ramseur (right) and his wife, Ellen Richmond (left). (ncmh)(loc)

held by southern gentlemen of his day. Like so many of his class in southern society, the most prominent of whom was Robert E. Lee, Ramseur was culturally, morally, and spiritually compelled by honor to defend his family, his community, and, just as important, his new nation."

The death of Lowell made a huge impact on Effie, who struggled with severe depression afterward. When she recovered, she became actively involved with helping the poor and disadvantaged in New York. She founded the New York City Charity Organization and became an inspiration for social reformers and, several generations later, feminists. It is interesting to think that Lowell's death provided her an opportunity to do more good than had he lived. Her work led the way for social reform and, ultimately, the women's movement.

At Lowell's funeral on October 28, 1864, the chaplain asked, "Are we paying too heavy a price for our country's freedom? Here if ever we might be permitted to say so, but here, beside these precious remains, our full hearts answer—no—not too much—not too much." He continued, "The price was a generation of men—a generation of mothers now sonless, sisters brotherless, wives husbandless, children fatherless."

In May of 1861, unaware of the truly dark days that lay ahead, President Lincoln wrote a letter to the parents of a fallen soldier. His letter serves as a reflection for the Lost Generation of our great Civil War. "In the untimely loss of your noble son," Lincoln wrote to Ephraim D. and Phoebe Ellsworth, "our affliction here, is scarcely less than your own. So much of promised usefulness to one's country, and of bright hopes for one's self and friends, have rarely been so suddenly dashed, as in his fall."

SHANNON MOECK *is a park ranger at Cedar Creek and Belle Grove National Historical Park. Her responsibilities include interpretation, research, volunteer management, webmaster, social media coordination, and assisting in the development of the park.*

"With Malice Toward None"

AFTERWORD

BY CHRIS MACKOWSKI

"Thank God that I have lived to see this!" Lincoln said. It was April 4, 1865. News had just reached him of the collapse of the Confederate line around Petersburg and Richmond and of Robert E. Lee's westward retreat with the Army of Northern Virginia. Already Ulysses S. Grant's armies were in pursuit. Lincoln was interested in what lay behind.

"It seems to me that I have been dreaming a horrid dream for four years," the president continued, "and now the nightmare is gone. I want to go to Richmond."

And go he did. That day, April 4, Lincoln landed at the city docks and took his son Tad—just turned twelve that day—on a walking tour of downtown. Thousands of freed slaves greeted them. So did the icy stares of Richmond's citizens. Miraculously, though, no one took a shot at him.

While making a stop at the home of his Confederate counterpart, Jefferson Davis, someone asked Lincoln what he intended to do about the vanquished Southerners. Lincoln replied that he didn't intend to issue specific orders on that score, but he made his wishes to the army clear: "If I were in your place, I'd let 'em up easy."

Lincoln had been sending such signals for weeks. During his Second Inaugural Address, delivered on March 4, his most famous passage outlined a vision "with malice toward none, with charity for all." In early May, the Abolitionist newspaper *The Liberator* would publish a Lincoln letter, written in July of 1862, in which the president vowed, "I shall do nothing in malice. What I deal with is too vast for malicious dealing."

On March 28, during a conference with Grant, Maj. Gen. William T. Sherman, and Rear Admiral David Dixon Porter aboard the steamer *River Queen*, Lincoln made sure his top commanders knew his mind.

Unveiled on April 5, 2003, a statue by sculptor David French depicts an intimate moment between father and son—Abraham and Tad Lincoln—during their visit to the fallen Confederate capital on April 4, 1865. The Lincolns' actual visit was far less quiet. (nps)

"What was to be done with the rebel armies when defeated?" Sherman asked him. "And what should be done with the political leaders, such as Jefferson Davis . . . ?"

Lincoln assured them he was ready. "All he wanted of us," Sherman recalled, "was to defeat the opposing armies, and to get the men composing the Confederate armies back to their homes, at work at their farms and in their shops."

Lincoln could not "speak his mind fully" on Davis, but he suggested that if Davis cleared out of the country altogether, it might be best for all involved.

Davis was trying to do just that when news reached him, on April 19, of Lincoln's assassination. Davis did not get the full details and at first wondered if it was a hoax—but soon he had the truth confirmed. Lincoln had been shot on the night of April 14 while attending a play at Ford's Theater and had died early the next day.

Inscribed at the Lincoln Memorial in Washington, D.C., Lincoln's vision can still serve as a call to noble action in troubled times. (kd)

"We felt his death was most unfortunate for the people of the Confederacy," recalled Confederate Postmaster General John Reagan, "because we believed it would intensify the feeling of hostility in the Northern States against us. . . ."

Indeed, Davis himself said, "I fear it will be disastrous to our people, and I regret it deeply."

In Raleigh, North Carolina, Sherman had been on his way to meet with his Confederate counterpart, Gen. Joseph E. Johnston, when word reached him of the assassination. It was the morning of April 17, some 48 hours after Lincoln's death. Sherman immediately understood the implications, and he ordered the news suppressed. It added a grim urgency to his discussion with Johnston.

"Lincoln was peculiarly endeared to the soldiers, and I feared some foolish woman or man in Raleigh might say something or do something that would madden our men," Sherman feared. If that happened, "a fate worse than Columbia would befall the place," he said, invoking the South Carolinian capital that his men had burned to the ground the past February.

Johnston worried along much the same lines, reportedly breaking into a visible sweat as he read the telegram when Sherman presented it to him. "[T]he event was the greatest possible calamity to the south," Johnston said.

Johnston's fears—and Davis's and Reagan's and countless others'—would bear out over time as Radical Republicans inflicted their revenge on the South through the unforgiving imposition of Reconstruction. A longtime political rivalry between Davis and the new president, Andrew Johnson, would give that revenge a personal edge.

But at Bennett Place Johnston and Sherman negotiated a wide and sweeping peace—one that, as it turned out, overstepped their bounds. Secretary of War Edwin Stanton, the *de facto* man in charge of the Federal government in the days immediately following Lincoln's assassination, was hardly in an expansive mood. He sent Grant to North Carolina to straighten out Sherman and secure Johnston's surrender under the same conditions Grant had offered Lee.

Though far less encompassing than Sherman's original terms, the terms Grant offered at Appomattox—and which Sherman and other commanders subsequently offered—were nonetheless magnanimous, particularly from a man who had once earned the nickname "Unconditional Surrender." In February 1862, Grant had forced the capitulation of Fort Donelson under "no terms except an unconditional and immediate surrender." On July 4, 1863, the Mississippi River citadel of Vicksburg fell under similar, though slightly less rigorous, terms.

At Appomattox on April 9, 1865, however, Grant offered to let Lee's men and officers keep their personal firearms. "[I] would be an unnecessary humiliation to call upon them to deliver their side arms," he later explained. He also let them keep their horses. Planting season was upon them, and those men would need their horses back on their farms even as they hammered their swords back into ploughshares.

Most importantly, Grant allowed Confederate soldiers, once given rations and paroled, to just simply *go home*. They were not treated like prisoners or criminals. They were, he reportedly said, fellow countrymen once more. Grant's charity directly reflected Lincoln's vision for peace.

"I knew his goodness of heart," Grant said of Lincoln in his memoirs, "his generosity, his yielding disposition, his desire to have everybody happy, and above all his desire to see all the people of the United States enter again upon the full privileges of citizenship with equality among all."

That the collapse of the Confederacy did not unravel into chaos, guerilla warfare, bushwhacking, and bloodshed is a testament to the power of Lincoln's belief in "the better angels of our nature." Alas, dark things would come in the months and years ahead, unfortunately—but in the closing days of the war, at least, Lincoln's lack of malice won out.

Lincoln lived to see that much—the end of his nightmare and the start of peace.

Thanks to his vision, thousands of others lived, too.

CHRIS MACKOWSKI, *Ph.D.,* *is the editor of Emerging* *Civil War and the author* *of a dozen books.*

Suggested Reading

THE SURRENDERS OF THE CONFEDERACY

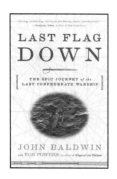

Last Flag Down: The Epic Journey of the Last Confederate Warship
John Baldwin and Rob Powers
Three Rivers Press, 2008
ISBN-13: 978-0307236562

A number of good accounts exist of the C.S.S. Shenandoah's final voyage, but Baldwin and Powers—a power writing duo—weave a gripping narrative that flows like a novel. Much of the book was based on the journals of the ship's executive author, an ancestor of Baldwin's.

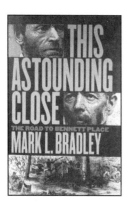

This Astounding Close
Mark Bradley
University of North Carolina Press, 2000
ISBN: 978-0807857014

The most detailed study of the surrender negotiations between Sherman and Johnston, Bradley is the recognized authority on the Carolinas campaign. The book takes readers from the aftermath of Bentonville through the multiple negotiations at the Bennett Place, to the final surrender of the Army of Tennessee. Bradley researched his topic thoroughly, making use of many previously unpublished sources.

The Appomattox Campaign
Chris Calkins
Schroeder Publications, 2008
ISBN: 978-1-889246-55-0

Regarded as the authority on the Appomattox campaign, Chris Calkins has published many works on the events of April 1865. This overview of the campaign includes excellent maps and many fascinating sidebars that shed light on little-known aspects of the campaign.

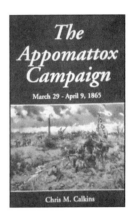

The Final Bivouac
Chris Calkins
H. E. Howard, 1988
ISBN: 978-0930919504

This work by Calkins delves into the fascinating but often-neglected details of the surrender. It chronicles events during the final days that troops were camped at Appomattox, such as the printing of paroles, the issuing of food and supplies, and the meeting of the commissioners. Each phase of the surrender process—infantry, cavalry, and artillery—is detailed.

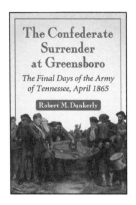

The Confederate Surrender at Greensboro
Robert M. Dunkerly
McFarland, 2013
ISBN: 978-0786473625

Drawing upon more than 200 eyewitness accounts, this is the first detailed study of the surrender of the Army of Tennessee, one of the most confusing, frustrating, and tension-filled of all the surrenders. Long overshadowed by Appomattox, this event was much more representative of how most Americans in 1865 experienced the conflict's end. The book includes a timeline, organizational charts, an order of battle, maps, and illustrations. It also provides information on Confederate campsites that have been lost to development and neglect.

The Collapse of the Confederacy
Mark Grimsley and Brooks D. Simpson, eds.
University of Nebraska Press, 2001
ISBN: 978-0803221703

This volume examines the ending of the war from many angles. It includes essays by various historians who analyze the military and political events of 1865 and discuss the options available to, and the decisions of, commanders and leaders on both sides. Factors such as morale, the home front, and strategies of negotiation are all explored in this volume.

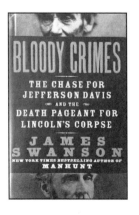

Bloody Crimes: The Chase for Jefferson Davis and the Death Pageant for Lincoln's Corpse
James L. Swanson
William Morrow, 2010
ISBN-13: 978-0061233784

For this tale of two presidents, it was the worst of times and it was the worst of times. Swanson juxtaposes the flight of Jefferson Davis after the collapse of Richmond against the funeral journey of Abraham Lincoln after his assassination. The conversation Swanson creates between the two events sheds fascinating insights into both.

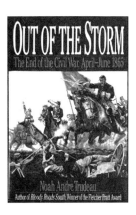

Out of the Storm
Noah Andre Trudeau
Little, Brown, and Co., 1994
ISBN 978-0316853286

Written in a unique day-by-day format, Trudeau's work follows events as they unfolded across the various theaters in the spring of 1865. His style of writing reveals insights into the actions of commanders and takes readers through the myriad of events in a novel-style format.

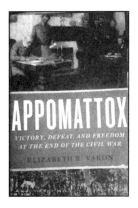

Appomattox
Elizabeth Varon
Oxford University Press, 2014
ISBN 978-0-19-1975171-6

This is Varon's fourth book on the Civil War, and she turns her attention to the correspondence between Lee and Grant in the days leading up to the surrender. Her examination sheds light on the thinking of both commanders, and how each perceived the negotiations. She also examines postwar attitudes and memories of the conflict and its ending. This is the most recent scholarship on how the two sides perceived Appomattox.

Fight and Survive!
Lady Elizabeth Watson
Jackson County Historical Society, 1996
ASIN: B000EBVNJM

This is the story of the Civil War in Jackson County, Arkansas, where many units were organized at the start of the conflict. It is also the only detailed study of events at the end of the war, including the surrender at Chalk Bluff and subsequent events at Jaksonport and Wittsburg. Although dated, it makes good use of primary sources and includes detailed information on local units.

About the Author

Robert M. Dunkerly, co-author of the Emerging Civil War Series book *No Turning Back: A Guide to the 1864 Overland Campaign*, is a historian, award-winning author, and speaker who is actively involved in historic preservation and research. He has spent years analyzing the final months of the war: He has worked at Appomattox Court House National Historical Park and is the author of *The Confederate Surrender at Greensboro*.

Bert is a Park Ranger at Richmond National Battlefield Park and currently serves as President of the Richmond Civil War Round Table. He also serves on the Preservation Committee of the American Revolution Round Table-Richmond.

Bert has visited more than 400 battlefields and more than 900 historic sites worldwide. He holds a degree in History from St. Vincent College and a Masters in Historic Preservation from Middle Tennessee State University. He has worked at nine historic sites, written seven books, and more than twenty articles. His research includes archaeology, colonial life, military history, and historic commemoration. When not reading or writing, he enjoys hiking, camping, and photography.